HR Tech Strategy

HR Tech Strategy

Revolutionizing Employee Experience
Through HR-Tech Synergy

Marlene de Koning

BEP

BUSINESS EXPERT PRESS

Leader in applied, concise business books

HR Tech Strategy: Revolutionizing Employee Experience Through HR-Tech Synergy

First published in 2024 by
Business Expert Press, LLC
222 East 46th Street, New York, NY 10017
www.businessexpertpress.com

ISBN-13: 978-1-63742-567-1 (paperback)
ISBN-13: 978-1-63742-568-8 (e-book)

Business Expert Press Collaborative Intelligence Collection

First edition: 2024

10 9 8 7 6 5 4 3 2 1

To my brothers, Willem and Wouter, whose unwavering support and inspiration have been instrumental in my life and in my career journey.

Description

Uncover the Future of Workplace Happiness and Effectiveness!

Dive into the pages of *HR Tech Strategy* and unlock the secrets of crafting an unparalleled employee experience that transforms organizations and propels them to new heights of success.

Forge the ultimate *HR Tech Strategy* for unrivalled effectiveness:

- ✓ Embrace the proven formula for aligning technology-driven employee experiences with exceptional business results.
- ✓ Understand how an engaged, motivated workforce translates into increased efficiency, innovation, and overall success.
- ✓ Unearth the untapped potential of a dynamic HR–IT partnership.
- ✓ Delve into real-world examples, showcasing the power of synergy between these two vital departments.
- ✓ Learn the art of harmonizing cutting-edge technology with human-centric HR strategies.

HR Tech Strategy **is not just a book; it is your ticket to becoming a pioneer in revolutionizing employee experience!**

Keywords

employee experience; HR tech; employee skills; hybrid working; people analytics; metaverse; generative AI; employee well-being; diversity, equity, and inclusion; fairness at work; ethics in AI; ethics at work; HR ethics; asynchronous work; work culture; personalized work; personalized employee experience; manager skills; ethical skills; digital skills; collaboration analytics

Contents

Acknowledgments

I have always been a fan of the proverb "if you want to go fast, go alone and if you want to go far, go together." This book is written thanks to a lot of knowledge sharing, inspiration and motivation of family members, friends, entrepreneurs, colleagues and former colleagues, human resources (HR) leaders, and my network. I would like to express my deepest gratitude to my family members, Edwin, Daan, Loes, Leona, and Han, whose unwavering support and belief in me have been the bedrock of my journey. Their constant encouragement and understanding have given me the strength to pursue my passion for writing this book.

To all the individuals who generously shared their insights and experiences through interviews, Paul Haarhuis, Jamie Fleming, Ido Shikma, Sandhna Chintoe, Alex Bertram, Alexander Stolze, Marieke van Beurden, Vivian Acquah, Melanie van Halteren, Richard van Tilborg, Albert Hoekstra, David White, and Joris van Hulzen. I am immensely grateful for their valuable contributions. Their willingness to share their expertise and perspectives has enriched the contents of this book and I am honored to have had the opportunity to learn from them.

I extend my sincere appreciation to the people who brought me inspiration and connections and the reviewers, Cecilia Liao, Bogdan Manta, Chris Gideon, Vanessa Hoen, Kseniia Golubnycha, Ton Rodenburg, and Laszlo Zala, who dedicated their time and expertise to provide invaluable feedback and suggestions. Their constructive criticism and thoughtful insights have played a pivotal role in shaping the final manuscript, and I am immensely grateful for their guidance.

Furthermore, I would like to acknowledge the customers and companies that have played a significant role in my professional development. Their trust, collaboration, and willingness to share their challenges and successes have been instrumental in expanding my knowledge and understanding of the tech-driven HR landscape. I am grateful for the opportunities they have provided me to learn, grow, and apply these learnings in the creation of this book.

Finally, I want to express my deepest appreciation to all the readers who will embark on this journey with me. Their interest and engagement in the subject matter inspire me to continue exploring and share insights into the transformative power of technology in the realm of HR.

Thank you for being part of this incredible adventure. Your contributions, support, and presence have made this book possible, and for that, I am eternally grateful.

Introduction

In today's fast-paced and interconnected world, technology has become an integral part of our daily lives, and the workplace is no exception. From the way we communicate and collaborate at work to the tools we use to get our work done, technology has transformed the employee experience in countless ways. With the rise of digital transformation and the adoption of new technologies, such as artificial intelligence (AI) and virtual and augmented reality, we are witnessing a new era in which technology is reshaping both the way we work and the way we experience work. It is important to understand the impact of technology on employee experience (both positive and negative) and how organizations can harness technology to create more engaging, productive, and fulfilling work environments.

The phrase "future of work" has gained prominence in the last few years, especially with the rise of automation, AI, and other technological advances that are rapidly transforming the nature of work and the job market. It refers to the evolving landscape of employment and the ways in which work will be performed in the coming years and decades. The term is used to describe a range of different trends and developments, including the changing skills and competencies required of workers, the growth of flexible and remote work arrangements, and the impact of technology on the workforce and the workplace. The term is also often used to discuss the implications of these changes and to consider what actions can be taken to ensure that workers are prepared for the challenges and opportunities of the coming years.

The changing world of work is being influenced not only by technology, but also by societal, political, and behavioral influences that will contribute to shaping the future in general. One of these is the demographic changes impacting the availability of workers and skills in society. For example, in China, in 2050, the average age will be 48, due to an increase in life expectancy and a decrease in family size. However, in Nigeria, in 2050, the average age will be 22. Shrinking working populations (like in China) and growing working populations (like in African countries such as Nigeria) and their associated different needs will influence how the future of work looks.

The needs and demands of employees are shifting, and the power will shift from the employer to the employee. This requires companies to redesign their organizations and prepare for this future. Organizations need to think about how to fulfill their employees' desire for flexibility. They also need to understand whether or not they have enough talent domestically and, if not, how they will attract talent or move their business to where the talent supply is the highest.

These are all existential questions for organizations that cannot be answered solely by technology. However, in this book, I focus on the technological impact and influence and how these can help organizations and their teams prepare for the changing world of work. My goal is to help organizations understand the beauty of technology, and sometimes the risks, and how these technologies can help employees and organizations thrive.

In every job, increasingly more technology is being introduced and used. Even a job that did not have any technological component 10 years ago is today likely to utilize a device, system, or algorithm. One of the examples I always like to share is the story of pest controllers and the nature of their job 20 years ago. Back then, employees themselves could choose the routes that they took through a city, take down necessary notes on paper, and hand them in at the office at the end of the day. Fast forward to today, where many cities have implemented a technological solution to track rats, requiring a pest controller to digitally enter all types of data regarding the whereabouts of rats, such as the height of the water in the city. These data points then can be used to predict plagues and dictate the work of the pest control worker. Lots of these types of changes happen quickly, and sometimes the training offered to employees is only a few-week-long online tutorial, which can be hard for employees, especially when organizations fail to explain the importance and the bigger picture of how this information is being used and what the impact is if the control worker is not sharing data or is incorrectly sharing data points. Not knowing the impact of the work, not having enough time to adapt to the new ways of working, and being expected to change work methods quickly, without a great adoption and implementation strategy (which differs per the needs of different groups of employees), can be very stressful for people. This is especially true for the generation longest at work, for whom these fast changes can be demotivating and stressful, which can have a negative impact on their well-being or even push them to give up entirely and opt for early retirement. With a shrinking working population, this is considered a risk. Strategizing for being an inclusive organization while keeping the well-being of employees in mind is advised, for all generations, when creating a new technology strategy.

The world of work has changed and is becoming more complex. Technology plays a big role and affects how people work and gain experience. When it puts stress on workers and inhibits their performance, technology can also have a negative impact on the world of work. Moreover, these changes have an impact not only on the people's jobs, but also on society as a whole.

The difficulty lies in the fact that technology is not an influence on its own. Rather, the foundational understanding of technology that varies between the multiple generations in the workforce adds to the complexity. Moreover, the differences in the reliability of Internet access around the globe create a disparity in foundational knowledge among the youngest generation, based on where someone was born and grew up. In addition, some organizations adopt new technology when it is being launched, which adds unnecessary complexity. Organizations should "begin with the end in mind." Technology and innovation is not a strategy on its own. It needs to address the priorities of the organization. Technology can contribute to and accelerate a business' success. When making technology part of a strategy, employees are more likely to see the benefits of the technology and how it contributes to the success of the individual, the team, and/or the organization. It is important for organizations to understand what makes it rewarding for employees to adopt the different technologies and change their behaviors. Organizations should strive to implement technologies that enable their employees to do their jobs better and help them to feel better when performing their jobs.

When driving strategic human resources (HR) in response to technological developments, HR departments should consider a variety of factors. In this book, I have covered some of the main challenges that organizations are facing and have highlighted technologies that can address these issues.

1. The HR department should consider how technological developments will affect the current workforce. This includes identifying the roles that may become obsolete or require new skills and determining how to address potential job displacement and training needs. HR should identify which new skills will be needed as a result of technological advancements and develop training and development programs to help employees acquire these skills. In Chapter 1, I will share more on the needs of different types of skills for an organization to thrive in the next decade. I will discuss not only the importance of hard and soft skills needed in the changing world of work but also the role of ethical skills. Ethical skills are important, both for establishing a moral strategy (for what purpose are we going to use the data?) and also when developing technologies (what data did we use? Is the algorithm developed inclusively? Do we understand why machine learning classifies things in a certain way?). These questions are all part of ethics, and having ethical skills is crucial in the changing world of work.

2. Since the COVID-19 pandemic, organizations have implemented increasingly more technologies that allow employees to work from home. The new hybrid way of working requires different policies from HR departments regarding communication and collaboration and the technologies that employees can use. In Chapter 2, I will share my vision on the advantage of strategizing for a more personalized employee experience over choosing one-size-fits-all technologies. Employees developed different kinds of needs when working from home, and some needs are seen as a right. However, these privileges should not prevent a team from reaching its goals and it should not cross boundaries set by the organization. Technology can help in facilitating this new way of working and help individuals, teams, and the organization to thrive—this too will be addressed in Chapter 2.

3. Organizations should address employee well-being as a response to technological developments in the changing world of work. While technology has many benefits, it can also lead to increased stress, burnout, and feelings of isolation. In Chapter 3, I will address well-being and how organizations can enable employees to cope with the demands of their work and maintain their mental and physical health. By addressing well-being, organizations can create a more positive work environment that increases productivity and creativity, enhances recruitment and retention efforts, and helps organizations to meet legal and ethical obligations.

4. Fairness is crucial when using or developing new technologies, because technology has the potential to impact employees' lives in significant ways. Technological advancements can lead to increased efficiency, productivity, and convenience, but they can also perpetuate existing inequalities and biases leading to unfair outcomes. The topic of fairness is addressed in Chapter 4, as to how technology can contribute to avoiding discrimination and ensuring equity within the organization. Fairness can help ensure that the technologies are designed in a way that avoids discrimination against any single group.

Throughout the first four chapters, I will reference different technologies and applications and address how they could be leveraged to address these as reflected in figure I.1. In the final two chapters, I will highlight two such technologies: people analytics and the metaverse.

1. Evidence-based decision making is important for organizations, and with the increasing availability of data and analytics tools in an organization, it can be applied. People analytics enables leaders and HR professionals to make informed decisions about their workforce. In Chapter 5, I address the importance of building and maintaining trust while using technologies (e.g., people analytics) and the importance of protecting employees' privacy. By leveraging data and analytics tools, organizations can make better-informed decisions about their most valuable assets, their employees.

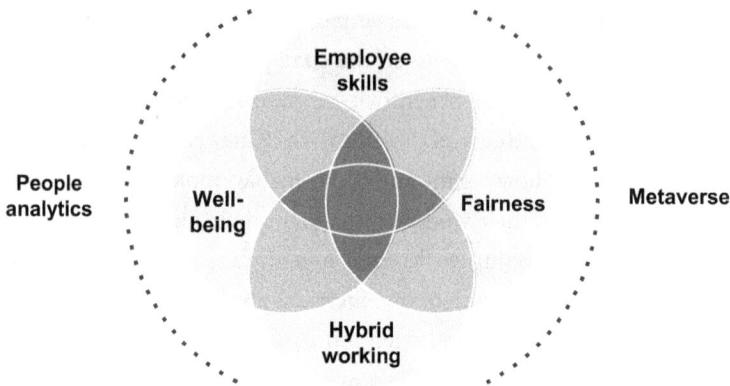

Figure I.1 Four business challenges and two supporting technologies

2. Mixed reality and the metaverse are emerging technologies that have the potential to transform the way that people work and collaborate. Understanding these technologies and their potential to address business challenges is crucial for organizations to stay ahead of their competition. Also, when organizations make the decision to not use some of these technologies, it should be a conscious choice and not because of a lack of understanding of the technology. Over the past few years, my customers' interest in the metaverse has sharply grown, reflected in the increasing number of conversations I have had with them on the subject. Accordingly, Chapter 6 is dedicated to the topic. Understanding the metaverse and mixed reality is important, because they can enhance remote work, improve learning and development, enable new forms of collaboration, and create new business opportunities. By leveraging these technologies, organizations can improve their productivity, creativity, and competitiveness in an increasingly digital world.

Since organizations do not know exactly which technological developments will affect their business operations, HR leaders have the opportunity to take on a strategic and facilitating role in introducing new technologies to grow their organization. Technological developments do not happen to companies. Conscious choices can be made about the type of technology and the way in which it is implemented, depending on an organization's strategy and the wishes of its employees. If an organization chooses to permanently focus on innovation, it is important that all employees are involved in this development. Without extra effort on the part of the HR department, there is a good chance that the older employees and the less educated will be left behind. HR should therefore pay active attention to include these groups in the innovation processes and in the realization of innovations within the organization.

In my career, I have worked mainly with two departments, IT and HR, and they both drive a different agenda. With more technology entering the workforce and the complexity it brings, there is a bridge needed between the two departments. HR departments need to understand not only more about technologies and innovations and how these both affect the workforce but also how these can be used to drive a more strategic HR agenda. IT should be aware of the impact that new technologies have on the workforce, the stress it can sometimes bring, and how it can be perceived as a burden, preventing the tools from being adopted and used within the organization. Implementing new technologies demands a change in how employees have always worked, and to be successful, organizations need to understand and drive the changes of both departments. HR and IT should collaborate, experiment, and learn together to bring optimal success to organizations.

CHAPTER 1

Employee Skills

There is a disconnect between the skills that employees have and the skills that are needed by an organization to stay ahead of their competition and continue to thrive in the changing world of work. Many reports explore the shortage of employees' skills or the earlier-said disconnect. Reports on the Great Resignation[*] and Great Reshuffle[†] only bolster this trend. The Great Resignation and Great Reshuffle are two related phenomena that have emerged in response to changes in the world of work, especially during the COVID-19 pandemic. With the labor market becoming increasingly tighter, these changes generate a great challenge.

For generations, we have experienced growth in the labor market, but this era of growth is over. Due to automation, the demand for labor has changed. The supply of labor is decreasing and is not fit for the purpose unless employees are reskilled or upskilled. Labor shortages will continue to exist for decades. Even with more women entering the workforce, a focus on attracting more immigrants, and the overall employment rate within the EU reaching its 75 percent target, there is still a shortage of

---

[*] The Great Resignation refers to the large number of employees who are leaving their jobs voluntarily. This trend began in 2021, as many employees reassessed their priorities and work–life balance in light of the COVID-19 pandemic. The Great Resignation has been seen across a wide range of industries and sectors from health care and retail to finance and technology.

[†] The Great Reshuffle refers to the broader changes in the job market that occurred during the COVID-19 pandemic. Many businesses shifted to remote work or hybrid models, which led to a greater demand for digital skills and increased competition for jobs in certain sectors. There was a shift in job demand, with many organizations looking for employees with experience in fields such as e-commerce, cybersecurity, and data analytics. Together, the Great Resignation and Great Reshuffle represent a significant shift in the labor market, with workers and companies adopting to new ways of working and changes in demand for certain skills.

skilled labor that continues to grow, not only in Europe but also globally. Urgent action is needed in developing digital skills for organizations to drive growth in a hybrid work environment. With this tight labor market and in the face of economic uncertainty, many organizations are struggling to find employees with the exact combination of skills and degrees required for a role. A McKinsey study showed that globally 375 million workers might have to change occupations in the next decade to meet companies' needs and that automation could free up employees to spend as much as 30 percent of their time on new tasks.[1] Changes in occupation demand different skills and require both the employee and the employers to invest in upskilling. It is interesting to consider what will come of the time the automation frees up for employees: will the employees like to spend that time on new work or will this time be spent more on leisure and learning?

Organizations will increasingly have to restructure to various degrees, to meet these challenges and stay competitive. This redesign of organizations influences the labor market and also the way that organizations train employees with the right knowledge and skills to be able to respond to the demands they face. Both organizations and employees are expected to deliver innovations in a dynamic globalizing and complex society—and expectations of organizations and its leadership are high. Organizations expect employees to use technology as soon as it is implemented to generate more productivity and that employees will be better at their jobs and happier.

However, the reality is that the employees who are supposed to work with these tools are not involved in the decision-making processes of buying. Thus, they do not always understand why they must use such new technologies or how they, their teams, or their company as a whole can benefit from them. Moreover, after acquiring new technologies, companies sometimes do not invest the necessary resources into ensuring the technologies' correct integration and use, which can lead to negative consequences. Barriers to adapting to such new technologies vary and include being skeptical, being afraid, or simply not knowing how to use a tool in a beneficial way. Employees are sometimes unaware that these tools even exist. This behavior can result in procrastination, as employees neglect completing online trainings, familiarizing themselves with the tools, and remembering particular login procedures. This can result in frustration for both the employer and the employee and lead to an overall negative experience.

There are different challenges on both the individual, and the organizational level. A skills gap addresses the demand for every employee to be more digitally educated in order to continue to perform their jobs and the new managerial skills that the leadership needs in order to build the right capabilities to innovate in this continuously evolving world of work.

Skills Gap

There is no such thing as a perfect labor market—one without incongruities between supply and demand. Such discrepancies translate into quantitative mismatches (shortages and surpluses) in the labor market, on the one hand, and qualitative mismatches (imbalances between the knowledge and skills of workers and the demands of the work), on the other hand; this is often referred to as a skills gap. There are various causes for mismatches between people and work, due to changes in labor market supply and demand. It is inevitable that the redesign of work will encompass many digital, technical, and even automated elements. For example, various technological changes and developments, such as artificial intelligence (AI), big data, and robotization, ensure that work and work content are constantly changing. Facing this acceleration in automation, people will be anxious about losing their jobs, and organizations will be nervous about losing their employees that have the right skills. Data from Gartner TalentNeuron™ indicates that, since 2017, the skills required to perform any given job have increased by 10 percent every year,[2] which has increased the need and motivation for organizations to either upskill or reskill their entire workforce.

Organizations need different types of skills than those offered by their current employees or jobseekers. This skills gap can be the result of ill-prepared candidates entering the workforce or the fact that technology changes at a mind-boggling pace and companies are not teaching or training their employees to keep up with arising changes.[3] To keep the match optimal, it is important, in a timely manner, to identify and anticipate risks of a mismatch occurring. Some employers struggle to fill jobs because of skills gaps, which sometimes occur due to unrealistic expectations set by employers. It is important to identify what skills employees need to do their jobs well, not only now but also in the future. It is also important to think about what innovations organizations invest in and how doing so will dictate what skills organizations will need to acquire in the coming years. In fact, a Deloitte report states that the global "skills gap may leave an estimated 2.4 million positions unfilled between 2018 and 2028, with a potential economic impact of $2.5 trillion."[4]

Knowledge Transfer

Transferring knowledge can be challenging, but there are several strategies that organizations can use to overcome this obstacle. The majority of my customers face the challenge of transferring knowledge for two main reasons: (1) they are dependent on contractors or (2) the average age of their employees is high. Organizations that depend upon contractors experience knowledge loss after a project is completed and a contractor leaves, taking along with them their knowledge, which has not been captured by the organization. The same challenge applies when organizations are confronted with a high average age among their employees and the occurrence of older, more experienced employees leaving the workforce without transferring all of the knowledge that they have accrued over their whole career.

There are apps and platforms available that pair an organization's less experienced employees with its more experienced ones, with the latter serving as mentors to transfer knowledge through direct and hands-on learning. Allowing employees to work in different roles within an organization can expose them to different types of knowledge. This is called job rotation, and it can also contribute to preventing skills gaps, if employees have already rotated before a shortage of skills exists in an organization. Creating communities or groups of employees who share a common interest or goal can also help facilitate the transfer of knowledge through informal interaction and collaboration.

Organizational network analysis (ONA) is a method that can be used to analyze the social networks and communication patterns within an organization. It can help in creating structured groups that are selected based on an organization's goals for knowledge transfer. Using technology to capture and share knowledge through databases, wikis, or other tools can help make the knowledge more accessible to others. A knowledge management system and even AI can be used to capture and share knowledge. It is important to note that transferring knowledge is a difficult and ongoing process. Organizations should continuously strive to find new ways and technologies to capture and share it.

Skills Passport

In the future, technological knowledge will become increasingly important. Complex analytical, cognitive, and empathic skills are becoming increasingly important for employees, as many standardized tasks have become automated. Many organizations assume that their skills gap is a result of hard skill shortages, but employees may also lack soft skills that the organization needs in order to thrive. With more automation and AI entering the workplace, ethical skills should, in my view, be one of the most important soft skills for all employees.

According to a McKinsey survey, over 50 percent of employees say that their employer does not understand their current capabilities.[5] Sometimes, employees move to a different position within the same organization and they do not need all of their acquired skills for their new job. These skills can be useful for a future role but are oftentimes forgotten by the organization. This results in (1) candidates being overlooked when internal mobility opportunities arise and (2) employers offering the wrong kinds of training, both of which leave employees feeling undervalued and disengaged.

One of the solutions to address the skills gap for individual employees could be a skills passport. A skills passport is a document that outlines an individual's education, training, and skills. It is designed to help individuals showcase their abilities and achievements to potential employers and stand out in the job market. While skills passports are mostly discussed in the context of external job market, I think they can also be used internally to address capability gaps and to create a more optimal internal mobility experience for both employer and employee. Some of the benefits in using a skills passport to address the skills gap are:

1. *Improved employability*: A skills passport helps individuals highlight their strengths and accomplishments, making them competitive in the job market. It can also help employers easily identify the skills and qualifications of potential hires, which makes it easy for them to find the right fit for their organization. It also helps to reduce bias in the hiring process by providing a standardized way for individuals to showcase their skills.

2. *Enhanced career development*: A skills passport can help individuals identify areas upon which they need to improve or for which they must acquire additional skills. It can also serve as a roadmap for career development, helping individuals set goals and plan their professional growth.

3. *Better alignment with company needs*: A skills passport can help employers identify and address skills gaps within their organization. By identifying the skills and qualifications of their current workforce, they can develop training and development programs to address any gaps and ensure that their employees have the skills needed to succeed.

Overall, a skills passport can be a valuable tool for individuals and organizations alike in addressing skills gaps and promoting career development. However, the challenge is that organizations need to classify what skills are needed for each role. This is an upfront investment that, if not given priority, could delay the optimal use of the technologies already available to them.

Another question that can arise when discussing skills passports relates to who owns the data and whether it can be transferred when an individual moves between organizations. Employees should own the content of their skills passports. That would allow the employee to determine which parts (if any) of the skills passport they want to share with their employer or third parties. Most of the current skills passport platforms containing skills data are made available by employers. The consequence is that an individual who changes employers loses access to their skills passport.

Moreover, it is not clear whether user data is optimally protected. In the privacy statements of existing platforms, it is not always possible to determine whether and how providers of skills passports handle user data. Employers see a risk in employees owning the data or allowing a skills passport to be transferred between organizations.

LinkedIn, in my view, has some elements of the skills passport. LinkedIn members do update their profile on a regular basis and keep their skills up to date. However, organizations are not always encouraging their employees to showcase their skills. When I was working at LinkedIn, many of my customers were afraid of encouraging their employees to create a LinkedIn profile. They thought it might lead to their employees finding a new job, because having a LinkedIn profile creates more visibility. If we look at all the reports on why people leave organizations, the cause is rarely because they receive opportunities that they cannot refuse, due to the increased visibility. Rather, the cause is related to their manager, a lack of development opportunities, flexibility, remuneration, and so on. The benefit of having employees' profiles on LinkedIn is that organizations can benefit from all of their employees' individual brands and networks to enhance their own. Overall, the benefits most of the time outweigh the risk of making employees think that they can leave. In an interview, the CCO of Timing Paul Haarhuis[‡] mentioned that when encouraging its clients to have their employees create skills passports, his company had experienced the same reaction that I had witnessed at LinkedIn with the profiles. This fear of organizations can be a factor of delay in the adoption and scale of a skills passport.

Luckily for the human resources (HR) department, the matching of skills can be automated. Automated skills matching and creating an automated skills passport make use of technologies such as AI and machine learning to analyze an individual's skills and qualifications and match them with job openings or career development opportunities. Those

---

[‡] Timing is an employment agency with 900 fixed information workers and 25,000 frontline employees. The company believes in the power of people who perform and are committed to the appreciation of frontline work. Every day, Timing employs more than 25,000 flex and payroll workers, from production workers to cleaners, ensuring that the Dutch economy continues to run. More at www.timing.nl.

technologies can help address skills gaps by providing an efficient and accurate way to identify the skills and qualifications of job candidates and match them with the right job opportunities.

Deciding who owns the data, standardizing systems so that skills can be exchanged, and creating support among both employer and employee remain challenges that we must overcome across industries before the skills passport will be adopted and implemented on a large scale and become a real success.

Once a skills gap is identified, there are several other technologies that can help address it by providing training and development opportunities for employees.

1. *Online learning platforms*: Online learning platforms such as Coursera, LinkedIn Learning, Pluralsight, and Udemy offer a wide range of courses and training programs on a variety of topics. These platforms allow employees to learn flexibly at their own pace, making it easier for them to acquire new skills and knowledge.

2. *Virtual reality (VR) training*: VR technology can be used to create immersive training experiences for employees. VR training can be used to teach practical skills, such as assembly line work and surgical procedures, as well as softer skills, such as communication and teamwork.

3. *Simulation software*: Simulation software allows employees to practice and test their skills in a simulated environment to gain hands-on experience without the risk of real-world consequences. This can be especially useful for training employees in high-risk industries, such as construction and aviation.

4. *AI-powered learning*: AI-powered learning systems can provide personalized training and development recommendations based on an individual's skills and goals. These systems can analyze an individual's performance and suggest areas for improvement, helping to close skills gaps.

AI-powered learning has been around for a while, but with new technologies entering the market, AI-powered learning gets more attention and might require more explanation to employees to help them understand how data is being used and for what purpose. An example of AI-powered learning is adaptive learning, which uses machine learning algorithms to personalize the learning experience for each employee. Adaptive learning systems analyze data on how individuals learn, their strengths and weaknesses, and their progress on learning the materials. Based on this analysis, the system adapts the content, pace, and difficulty level of the learning material to meet the needs of each student. Another example of AI-powered learning is intelligent tutor systems. These systems use AI and machine learning algorithms to simulate the behavior of a human tutor. AI-powered learning can provide personalized and adaptive learning experience to employees in ways that in-person trainings cannot bring, helping employees to achieve their learning goals more effectively and efficiently.

Creating learning paths that are beneficial for employees can include different learning methodologies and platforms. Having to utilize many platforms at once without the ability to track the full development of online, virtual, and offline learning can make the experience for both the employer and the employees suboptimal. Offering learning paths through a central learning experience platform such as Degreed or Viva Learning can enhance the overall employee learning experience.

In general, these technologies can help employees acquire new skills and knowledge and, at the same time, help employers ensure that their workforce has the skills needed to succeed in the current and future job markets.

Case: Skills Matching to Uncover Hidden Talents

Many organizations focus mainly on external recruitment. As such, it is likely that an organization's own employees are being recruited by their competitors, as, simultaneously, the organization's own recruiters are looking for talent externally. A departing employee is very costly for an organization, due to loss of productivity, the impact on the affected team (higher workload and mental impact), and the costs of recruiting and onboarding a new employee. Internal mobility could, therefore, be beneficial in many ways for an organization. However, it is difficult that many organizations do not know

(Continues)

(*Continued*)

the skills that its employees hold, which sometimes make it easier for employers to look externally.

Skillzilla is an initiative that Timing offers to its customers to help them uncover hidden talents within their organization. One of Timing's customers had a manager looking to hire a lab technician, and the vacancy had been open for a long period of time. The manager could not find the right candidate and did not think that he could fill the vacancy internally. When hiring an expensive external agency did not result in the right candidate, the customer created skills profiles for its employees. It turned out that one of the production workers was a migrant worker who was a lab technician in his home country. As it turned out, the organization and manager did not to know of this past experience and would not have discovered it, had they not used the skills assessments. This example is not an exception, and there are many parties that can benefit from such automatic skills assessments and matches.

Despite HR professionals being convinced that a skills-oriented market is part of the future of work, many of them do not know how to approach the topic. Defining all of the skills for all the roles within an organization can be time consuming. That is why it is very important to create awareness across an organization and leverage those technologies and tools that can help with defining all the skills. Skillzilla is a great example of such a tool, and it is being used by Timing's customers for mapping the skills of their frontline workers. Overall, it allows each organization to save time and other resources.

Another important component for which Skillzilla offers a solution is making employees aware of what is being offered internally. It regularly occurs that an organization has great potential, but that its employees are simply uninformed and their skills and ambitions are uncovered only when they have already decided to leave the organization to seek growth externally. While opportunities might also have been available internally, the employees simply were not aware. Skill profiles can be a starting point for conversations about growth within an existing role and career development opportunities.

The Importance of Ethical Skills

Ethical skills refer to the ability to make ethical decisions and conduct oneself in an ethical manner. These skills involve being able to identify ethical dilemmas, understand ethical principles and values, and apply them to all kinds of situations. Developing ethical skills is crucial in relation to the future of work. As technology advances and workplaces become more complex, ethical decision making becomes more challenging. It is essential to develop ethical skills to navigate these complexities and make decisions that are in line with ethical principles. As automation and AI continue to replace human labor, ethical skills become more important. Humans are responsible for programming and designing these systems, and it is essential to ensure that the systems are designed and implemented in an ethical manner. For employees, it is important to know that employers handle this process in an ethical manner, to be sure that they are treated fairly. For organizations, the proper design and implementation are very important for their reputation. In today's digital age, reputations can be easily tarnished by unethical behavior. Developing ethical skills is crucial in the future of work to navigate increasing complexity, diversity, automation, social responsibility, and reputation. I will be sharing more about ethics in Chapter 4.

The Need for Role-Specific Skills

Frontline Worker Skills

There are a number of ways that technology can be leveraged to upskill or reskill frontline workers. VR and augmented reality (AR) training can be used to simulate real-world scenarios and environments, allowing frontline workers to practice and develop skills in a safe and controlled setting. This can be particularly useful for training in industries such as retail, manufacturing, construction, and health care.

Automation and AI can be used to automate repetitive tasks, allowing frontline workers to focus on more complex and higher-value work. By leveraging digital tools, such as knowledge management systems, frontline workers can quickly access and learn from their organization's digital library of information and procedures. This helps employees to easily follow their organization's guidelines and increase efficiency. Frontline workers can also use remote monitoring and collaboration tools to connect with other team members and experts both inside and outside of the team. Such tools can help not only with learning but also with trouble shooting issues in real time. One example of how AI can be used to automate repetitive tasks is in the field of customer service. Many organizations now use AI-powered chatbots or virtual assistants to handle routine customer inquiries, such as answering frequently asked questions, processing simple requests, and providing basic information about products or services. These chatbots can be programmed to understand natural language, respond to customer inquiries, and provide high-level support to customers. Additionally, AI-powered chatbots can operate 24/7, providing customers with around-the-clock access to basic information and support, which can lead to increased customer satisfaction and loyalty, while also reducing the workload and stress of human customer service representatives. The time that is freed up by reducing repetitive tasks is then used for more complex customer service tasks.

Mobile learning can help frontline workers to access training materials and complete assignments from anywhere, including their privately owned mobile devices. This flexibility helps to facilitate accessibility to the learning process. An example of mobile learning for frontline workers could be a training program delivered through a mobile app that is accessible on their (own or shared) smartphones or tablets. The program could include interactive modules that teach employees how to perform specific tasks or follow certain procedures, such as proper cleaning and sanitation protocols or safety procedures in a hazardous work environment. Imagine a food processing company where frontline workers are responsible for ensuring that the products are handled and processed in a safe and hygienic manner. The company could develop a mobile app that contains a series of training modules on food safety and hygiene with interactive videos, quizzes, and games to make the learning process engaging and enjoyable. The employees could access these trainings through their mobile devices that they carry with them throughout the workday, which would allow them to learn on the go, without having to leave their work area or attend in-person training sessions. The mobile app could also include tracking and reporting features, allowing managers to monitor the progress of the team and its individuals to ensure that the required training is completed.

It is important to note that it is not just frontline workers who need to be upskilled, but managers and the leaders also need to be trained on how to use these technologies and tools to train their teams and measure their progress.

Case: Training Employees With Mixed Reality

When I interviewed Jamie Fleming, the founder and CEO of Altoura,[§] he shared an example of the creation of a virtual store by his company for one of its customers, Sprint Retail. The customer's intent was to use mixed reality for the layout of all of its products for all of its stores. Altoura's team created a virtual store, where all of the products were shown and could be virtually moved inside the store.

When the Altoura team showed the virtual store to the corporate IT team of Sprint Retail, learning and development (L&D) team was also present and later developed a transformative and innovative skills and training initiative. In the past, the L&D team trained employees in physical stores, to create an understanding of where the products are and how to address customer questions. The physical training helped build the muscle memory that is needed to deliver optimal customer service. The requirement for physical training resulted in the L&D team's traveling and being on the road for over 300 days a year to train all of the employees in every region. Training also had to be after hours, because it could not occur when the stores were open and customers were present. Ultimately, the L&D team began to use mixed reality not only for designing store layouts but also for actually training employees in a virtual store.

(Continues)

[§] Altoura is the pioneer of interactive digital twin technology and the maker of a productivity platform for spatial work. Altoura's no-code platform imports and transforms 3D assets into immersive, interactive, and collaborative spatial workflows, such as immersive training and design visualization. More at www .altoura.com.

(*Continued*)

> This technological application provided a huge opportunity to use 3D models to increase different productivity workstreams, and it allowed for the simulation of experiences in the physical world by allowing various parties to "be together" in a store while not actually being physically present. Moreover, the simulation increased the scale of the trainings and improved the well-being of the L&D employees by decreasing the need to travel. In addition, this type of training proved sustainable and more cost efficient. Overall, it was a success for the individual employees that were in need of training, the teams that created and offered the training, and the organization. This is an example in which technology had a positive impact on employee experience and created a win–win–win situation.

Manager Skills

Work is changing, and changes such as hybrid work require new skills from managers. Bad management results in poor talent retention, so reskilling on the management level is needed. When moving to a hybrid and more digital working environment, managers may need to develop new skills to effectively lead and manage remote and in-person (i.e., colocated) teams.

Soft Skills

Managers need to be able to adapt to the varying needs of remote and in-person team members and to create a work environment that supports both. They also need to be able to effectively communicate with team members who are working remotely and ensure that both in-office and remote employees are equally aware of expectations. Instant messaging and e-mail can easily include all parties, but video conferencing can prove challenging, because it can be difficult for remote employees to keep up with conversations that are occurring in person in a conference room.

When employees are not in the same location, it can be hard to read body language or facial expressions. One way to make it easier for everyone to read facial expressions is for all parties to turn on their individual cameras, even those who are present in the conference room. Managers must also learn to trust their remote employees and avoid micromanaging by continuously expecting employees to respond to chats or be visible online. They need to give remote employees the autonomy that they need to work productively and need to find new ways to keep employees engaged and motivated. Managers also need to be sensitive to the cultural differences and backgrounds of remote workers and be aware of how they may impact communication and work styles (e.g., some employees may prefer to work collaboratively or independently) regarding what the employees expect from their manager and how they choose to communicate with their manager. Finally, to create long-lasting success for a hybrid team, it is very important to manage the workload of remote employees, especially if they are working across time zones.

Hard Skills

Managers need to be familiar with the tools and technologies that remote team members use, such as virtual meeting platforms and project management tools, and be able to use those tools and technologies themselves to collaborate effectively. Organizations need to consider that the hybrid workplace of the future will be underpinned by technological, cloud-enabled devices and applications to support operations, collaboration, and employee experience. With technology supporting every facet of business, it is no surprise that digital skills will become the critical currency of the future workplace. Particularly for managers and leaders, there is an opportunity to address digital skills gaps through providing different kinds of technologies, for example, low-code/no-code platforms. These platforms require limited-to-no software programming skills and could empower all employees, including managers and leaders, with digital capabilities, regardless of their background or experience with technology. CBI reports that 29 percent of businesses claim to be investing in manager training to support the roll-out of hybrid working.[6]

Skills for Human Resources

Many of the readers of this book are HR professionals. Therefore, I find it beneficial to share the skills expected from HR teams as they prepare for the future of work. HR teams play a critical role in shaping the future of work by recruiting, developing, and retaining talent as well as fostering a positive and inclusive work environment. As such, HR teams will need to develop several key skills to effectively support the future of work.

Soft Skills

HR teams will need to be able to adapt quickly to changing organizational needs and workforce trends and technologies. A focus is needed on creating an engaging, fair, and inclusive work environment. HR teams will also need to be committed to promoting diversity and inclusion within the workplace and to be able to design and implement the right tools and technologies to support their new strategies. All of the implemented tools and technologies need to equally support both the remote and in-office employees. Moreover, HR professionals need to be willing to experiment with new and innovative practices and to move away from one-size-fits-all solutions and embrace a more personalized employee experience.

Hard Skills

HR teams need to be proficient in using digital tools and platforms, such as applicant tracking systems, e-learning platforms, and employee engagement software. Paramount are digital skills, including the use of cloud-based technologies and the implementation of a foundation of platforms and services that enable connection and collaboration throughout an organization. Developing these at all levels of an organization is a critical focus for learning leaders.

HR teams will need to be able to analyze and interpret data to make informed decisions about recruitment, training, and retention. Data can be used through the entire employee life cycle to increase employee experience. Many HR teams already have analytics and descriptive data available, but predictive and prescriptive data will become indispensable when focusing on phenomena such as burnout prevention. More details are included in Chapter 5.

HR teams should be ready to adapt and utilize technology to streamline and improve HR processes, allowing them to focus on more strategic work. The pace of technology is changing so rapidly that businesses need to reskill their employees at a faster rate to meet their needs. HR teams will play a vital role in developing and implementing learning and development (L&D) programs that support this reskilling process. L&D teams that create or support processes for learning in mixed reality or a metaverse will need expertise on immersive and 3D design, tools, and platforms, including game engines or 3D design platforms. L&D teams and their leaders will need to deepen their understanding of emergent technologies such as AR and VR.

Figure 1.1 visualizes the most important hard and soft skills mentioned in this chapter and the importance of ethical skills for both HR and leaders of an organization. It is worth noting that since the future of work is undetermined and uncertain, HR teams will have to be ready to adapt and evolve their skills to meet the needs of their organizations.

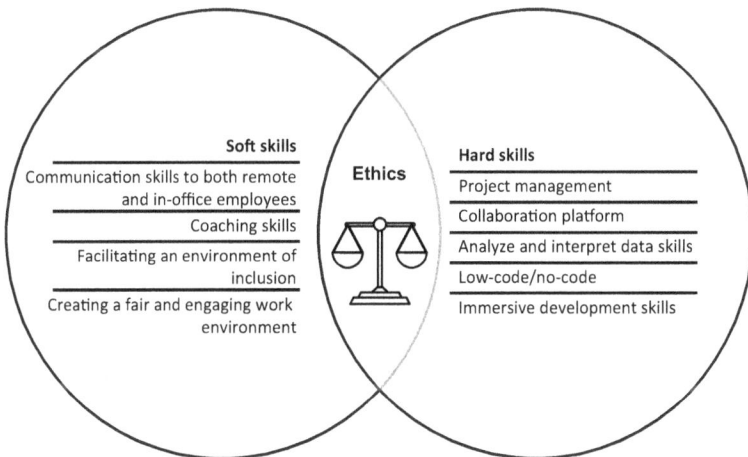

Figure 1.1 Soft and hard skills and the importance of ethical skills in both domains

Organization

In the past, organizations preferred to hire new employees in order to close skills gaps, but with shortages in the labor market and all organizations seeking the same talent, this past approach can no longer be the only strategy. Developing current employees is needed to close skills gaps, and as an added benefit, this approach is also more affordable. As a bonus, investing in the development of current employees also increases engagement; the main reason people leave their companies is due to a lack of growth and development, according to the 2022 LinkedIn Workplace Learning Report.[7] Therefore, it is important to invest in skills, talent, and employee strengths both within and outside of an organization to facilitate the transition from human capital management** to human capability management.[††,8] HR managers and business leaders need to acquire relevant knowledge about the available skill pool both inside and outside of an organization to facilitate sustainable matching and talent inflow within the network of organizations. To ensure that employees can remain enthusiastic, creative, and productive for longer, it is desirable that organizations not only invest in the knowledge and competencies of the employees but also pay attention to their well-being and creativity.

During my years at LinkedIn, the company launched the Economic Graph, a digital representation of the global economy based on LinkedIn's data of more than 875 million members, 59 million companies, 11 million job listings, 36,000 defined skills, and 129,000 schools. Through mapping every member, company, job, and school, LinkedIn is able to spot trends, including the most in-demand skills per region. These insights can help organizations and governments to understand the

---

** Human capital management is a more traditional approach that emphasizes the investment in people as assets that generate a return on investment (ROI). It focuses on recruiting, developing, and retaining employees with the right skills, knowledge, and experience to achieve business goals. Human capital management is primarily concerned with maximizing the productivity and efficiency of employees in order to achieve organizational objectives.

†† Human capability management is a more modern approach that emphasizes the development of human potential as an end in itself. It is based on the idea that individuals have unique talents, skills, and abilities that can be nurtured and developed to enhance performance and contribution to the organization. Human capability management is more concerned with creating an environment where employees are empowered to achieve their full potential and where their contributions are valued and recognized.

talent market and how to connect talent to opportunities.[‡‡] During the COVID-19 pandemic, many people lost their jobs, while other vacancies could not be filled due to high demand and a limited population possessing particular desired skills. Microsoft, GitHub, and LinkedIn launched the Global Skilling Initiative to address digital skills shortages by sharing free learning resources to help people train for and secure jobs.[9] This is one example of a skilling initiative, but more initiatives are happening on both the industry and regional levels. These overarching initiatives are needed since some skills gaps are a societal and not only an organizational challenge.

Hiring and developing employees with the needed skills is not sufficient. Organizations need to make sure that knowledge is not lost when employees decide to leave the organization and when working with contracted employees. It is important not only to understand who possesses what type of knowledge but also to collect and protect this knowledge. AI tools can help in classifying who within an organization possesses knowledge on what topics and in collecting and protecting this information. Such a process prevents a loss of knowledge when contractors fulfill their contracts and leave or when employees resign. ONA can be useful in creating human networks that help to understand the impact of strong and weak ties on the diffusion of knowledge. More information on ONA can be found in Chapter 5.

Today, organizations should start building new strategies, exploring the potential of new products and services, and training their managers and executives on the technologies that will soon be fundamental to their business. As generative AI, and metaverse and other mixed-reality technologies continue to mature, the companies that are prepared and willing to experiment with these new platforms and data structures will be the ones that define the next generation of digital business. Employers who are looking to create metaverse experiences will require 3D artists, game designers, and experts of the platforms upon which they plan to build. Just as enterprises in the 1990s, when the Internet became part of doing business, needed to hire professionals such as interaction designers and software engineers to execute their digital transformations, employers

---

[‡‡] www.linkedin.com/showcase/linkedin-economic-graph/.

nowadays will need to acquire the new set of skills required to thrive in a future driven by AI, metaverses and mixed reality. Organizations can start by identifying where they expect to compete as an enterprise and what skills gaps will prevent them from successfully executing those strategies. Developing a pipeline for new talent will be a long-term effort that should nevertheless begin today. In the interim, employers and managers should explore upskilling existing employees and building familiarity and skills with generative AI, and the metaverse and mixed-reality platforms that they intend to use.

Employers cannot expect this to be a one-time adjustment, but rather they need to embed a culture of learning within their organization. Remote and hybrid work might provide the new generation entering the workforce few opportunities to learn through observation, unless management is trained on and continuously aware of facilitating observational knowledge transfer. If a culture of learning can be established, it will also support employees to upskill, ensure that their capabilities remain relevant to the organizations' strategic ambitions, and allow internal advancement and mobility. Moreover, it will support leadership teams and IT professionals in harnessing technology to enable continuous transformation.

Thus, urgent action is needed not only for organizations, but also for their employees, to help them learn, reinvent, and grow with the pace of change. Moreover, our society as a whole can benefit by better matching individuals' skills to the jobs available in the new world of work.

Case: Building a Skills Organization at a Large European Bank

For established organizations that have been focused on other parts of the business, transitioning into a skills-focused and skills-enabled organization can be a challenge. Many organizations still expect learning to happen in the employees' own time and offer suboptimal learning platforms. Encouraging employees to learn beyond the compliance learning and offering a personalized employee experience can be difficult if not embedded in an organization's policies and processes. In an interview with a global head of L&D at a large European bank, I discussed the effects that changing toward a skills-focused and skills-enabled organization had on her department's workforce. Figure 1.2 explains the process her department undertook to reach the personalized learning experience. Currently, most of the employee experiences at many organizations are a one-size-fits-all and not personalized. A personalized learning experience is one factor in creating personalized employee experience.

As shown in Figure 1.2, before starting a transition, it is important to identify what skills already exist within an organization, what the potential legacy systems[§§] are, what the critical segments are within the business, and what current and future skills are needed for the organization.

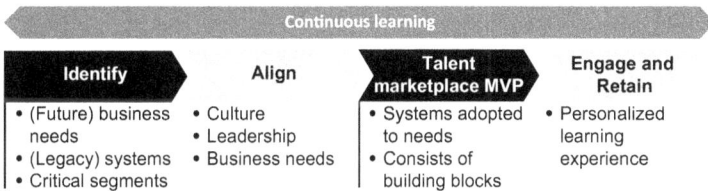

Continuous learning

Identify	Align	Talent marketplace MVP	Engage and Retain
• (Future) business needs • (Legacy) systems • Critical segments	• Culture • Leadership • Business needs	• Systems adopted to needs • Consists of building blocks	• Personalized learning experience

Figure 1.2 Steps to reach personalized learning experience

After the needs and systems are identified, the next phase is the alignment phase, where the learning needs must be aligned to the culture of the organization, the leadership priorities, and the business needs.

There are different challenges that need to be overcome when moving toward a personalized learning experience. Such a transition requires a different learning culture and includes a transformation

(Continues)

[§§] A legacy system is an outdated or obsolete computer system, software application, or technology that is still in use by an organization due to various reasons, such as costs or complexity of replacement, lack of available alternatives, or regulatory compliance requirements.

(*Continued*)

of leadership behaviors. Within an organization, different leaders face different challenges that could be related to growth and development, such as digital skills shortages and retention issues. Within each team, there can be different generational dynamics. Generational dynamics refer to the different attitudes, behaviors, and values that individuals from different generational cohorts bring to a team. At the moment, there are five generations present at the workforce: traditionalists, baby boomers, Generation X, millennials, and Generation Z. Each generation has its unique set of experiences and cultural influences that shape its perspectives, expectations, and workstyles. For instance, traditionalists tend to value hard work, loyalty, and authority while millennials and Generation Z prioritize work–life balance, flexibility, and a sense of purpose. These generational differences can lead to conflicts or misunderstanding within a team, especially if team members are not aware of or do not appreciate these differences. Effective leaders should be able to recognize and understand generational dynamics within their teams and use understanding to foster collaboration, respect, and understanding among team members. By valuing and leveraging each team member's strength regardless of their generation, teams can achieve great productivity, innovation, and success.

When implementing a personalized learning experience, it is important not only to understand the business needs and have support of the leadership, but also to understand that different generations prefer different methods for learning and development. Moreover, the overall program needs to fit within the culture of the organization.

The third phase is to start with a minimum viable product (MVP) that consists of multiple building blocks that are tailored to the different needs of an organization or department, which allows the team to be more flexible to quickly adapt to future needs. These building blocks can then feed into the final platform that offers a personalized learning experience and affects the overall personalized employee experience.

Conclusion

With technology supporting every facet of business, it is no surprise that digital, technical, and ethical skills will become a critical currency of the future workplace. Organizations need to strategize to hire, develop, and retain knowledge from within. New tools and technologies are constantly being developed that help organizations safeguard their skilled employees who help them become market leaders.

The importance of employees' skills, particularly ethical and digital skills, cannot be overstated in today's rapidly evolving business landscape. Companies that invest in developing their employees' skills in these areas are more likely to be successful and maintain their market leadership positions. Ethical skills are essential in ensuring that employees make the right decisions in situations that involve ethical dilemmas and to ask the right questions when leveraging AI.

Digital skills are critical in today's digital era, where technology is rapidly changing how we work and how we do business. Organizations that invest in developing their employees' digital skills are better equipped to adapt to technological advancements and capitalize on new opportunities presented by digital transformation. Moreover, companies that foster a culture of continuous learning and skill development are better positioned to attract and retain top talent. This not only enhances employee engagement and satisfaction, but also ensures that the organization has the necessary skills and expertise to remain competitive and agile in a constantly evolving business environment.

CHAPTER 2

Hybrid Work

As we navigate the post-COVID pandemic era, hybrid work has emerged as a popular model for organizations seeking to balance the benefits of in-person collaboration with the flexibility and autonomy of remote work. According to reports on the future of work and employee experience, hybrid work as a trend is often mentioned. LinkedIn claims that in March 2020, 1 in 67 U.S. jobs companies offered a remote work option. By the start of 2022, that number was about one in six.[1] Moreover, on LinkedIn, remote jobs attract 2.6 times more views and nearly 3 times more applicants than in-house jobs, as shown in Figure 2.1.

Hybrid work was already a reality in some organizations, but during the COVID-19 pandemic, many information workers and their employers were forced to go from working full time in an office to working fully remotely. After more than two years of fluctuating between being fully in the office and fully remotely, employees and thus their employers are in need of a hybrid working model. The panic surrounding hybrid and remote work has mostly subsided, but tensions remain between leaders and employees, with the former advocating for more time spent in the office and the latter pushing for greater flexibility. Even with more companies investing in their digital transformation, not many utilize an advanced hybrid work strategy, which could become a differentiating factor for companies to stay competitive. A hybrid working model requires an entirely new way of working. Developing such a model is not a matter of simply replicating the old way or prepandemic way of working in a digital form. Organizations that embrace a true hybrid work strategy, by reinventing the way work is done digitally while at the same time respecting successful work strategies of the past, will create a competitive advantage for many years to come.

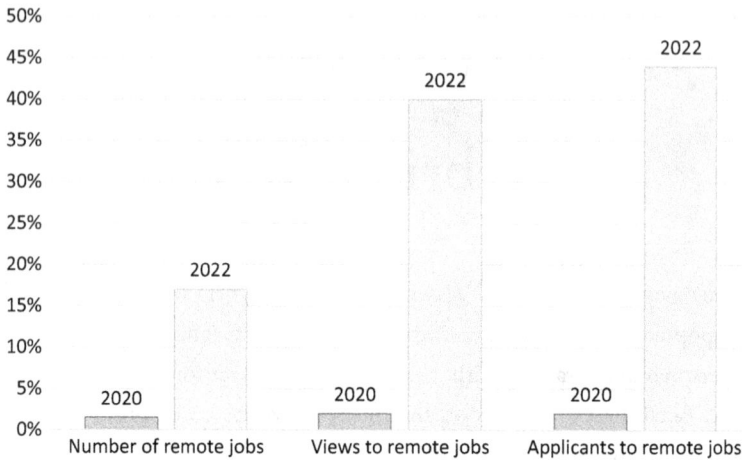

Figure 2.1 **Attractiveness of remote jobs based on LinkedIn data**

The tension between leaders and employees is referred to as "productivity paranoia."[2] Productivity paranoia refers to the disconnect between employee and employer on whether a hybrid environment enhances or negatively impacts productivity. This paranoia, in relation to hybrid working, can stem from the different perspectives and priorities that each group has. On the one hand, leaders may see hybrid working as a way to increase productivity, reduce costs, and improve the work–life balance of employees. On the other hand, they may also be concerned about maintaining control over their workforce, ensuring that employees work effectively, and maintaining a consistent company culture. At the same time, employees may view hybrid work as an opportunity for greater flexibility, autonomy, and work–life balance. They may be concerned about maintaining their privacy and having control over their work environment. They may also be concerned about the potential for decreased social interaction, feelings of isolation from colleagues, and how visible they are to their leaders.

The tension between leaders and employees in this context can lead to misunderstandings, conflicting expectations, and decreased satisfaction for both groups. Companies that try to revoke hybrid and remote work opportunities will be met with resistance, which can lead to increased attrition. Forrester predicts that 4 in 10 hybrid working companies will try to undo anywhere work—and fail.[3] In order to avoid this, leaders and employees need to have open and honest conversations about their expectations and priorities and find ways to balance the needs of both groups. The focus of HR leaders will be on the best conditions for their organizations, ensuring (1) equal treatment of employees, regardless of where they are working; (2) fair compensation; (3) productivity; and (4) a strong work culture. To ensure such conditions, HR leaders must set clear guidelines for hybrid working, providing the necessary tools and support for remote and hybrid work, and guarantee that employees have opportunities for social interaction and collaboration. With open communication and a focus on collaboration, leaders and employees can work together to create a successful and sustainable hybrid work environment. Most organizations will focus on refining the experience for the workforce. Companies that are more likely to succeed in the future will leverage flexibility as a core talent attraction and retention strategy, which will lead to improved cultural health and financial performance.

What Is a Hybrid Work Strategy?

For individuals, hybrid work refers to working part of the time in the office and part of the time from somewhere else. For organizations, hybrid can also refer to having a mix of fully on-site and fully off-site employees. A hybrid workplace model combines in-office and remote workers, where, during any given week, employees may split their time between coming into work on-site and working from home or a partner's or customer's location. This approach allows organizations and their employees to take advantage of the benefits of both remote and in-person work. Such an approach can be customized to meet the needs of different employees and teams. This customization allows leaders to strategize for a more personal employee experience, but at the same time such an arrangement also creates complexity.

Not every company is at the same stage of reaching a true hybrid strategy. Figure 2.2 shows the five stages that lead to the adoption of a true hybrid strategy.

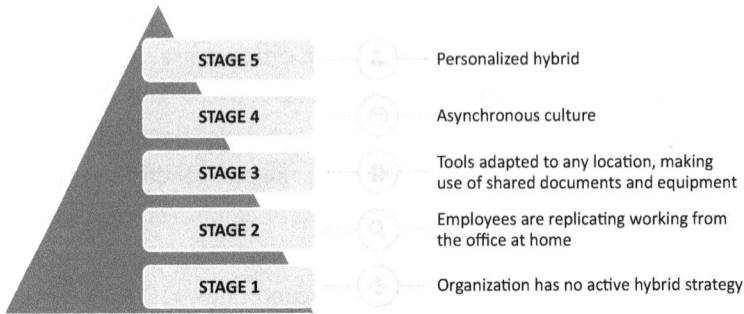

STAGE 5		Personalized hybrid
STAGE 4		Asynchronous culture
STAGE 3		Tools adapted to any location, making use of shared documents and equipment
STAGE 2		Employees are replicating working from the office at home
STAGE 1		Organization has no active hybrid strategy

Figure 2.2 Stages for a hybrid work strategy

Stage 1: Organization Has No Active Hybrid Strategy

In stage 1, where organizations have no active hybrid work strategy, employees are encouraged to work in the office and there is no real hybrid strategy or tools that support employees to work remotely. An organization that has no hybrid work strategy may face a number of challenges. Without a hybrid work strategy, employees may not have the option to work from home or other remote locations, which can limit their flexibility and work–life balance. Employees may also feel that the organization is not adapting to their needs or taking advantage of new technologies and, as a result, they may become disengaged and less productive. With an increasing number of organizations offering flexible work options, a lack of hybrid work strategy can make it more difficult for an organization to attract and retain top talent. Without a hybrid work strategy, an organization may struggle to effectively coordinate and manage its workforce, leading to inefficiencies and decreased productivity.

Stage 2: Employees Are Replicating Working From the Office at Home

Stage 2 does allow employees to work from home, but does not offer a change in working style compared to working in office. In this stage, employees are simply replicating their work habits but from their home office. Starting to replicate the work that used to be done in the office from home can offer some benefits. Working from home increases flexibility and gives employees more control over their work schedules, which can help them balance work and personal commitments better. Employees who work from home can be more productive than those who work in the office. This may be due to reduced distractions, more comfortable work environments, and fewer interruptions. Commuting to the office can also be very stressful, especially with long travel times and rush-hour traffic. Allowing employees to work from home can reduce this stress and create a more relaxed working environment.

There can also be a number of downsides to employees replicating in-office working habits while working remotely or in a hybrid working environment. Without clear boundaries between work and personal time, employees may find that they are unable to take breaks, engage in physical activity, or socialize with friends and family, which can lead to decreased physical and mental well-being. If employees are working longer hours and not taking regular breaks, their productivity and effectiveness can decrease, and they may experience decreased motivation and engagement. Moreover, the constant pressure to be productive and available can lead to increased stress and anxiety. In order to address these downsides, employees should be encouraged to develop healthy working habits that support their well-being, including taking regular breaks, setting boundaries between work and personal time, and engaging in physical activity.

Stage 3: Tools Adapted to Any Location, Making Use of Shared Documents and Equipment

Compared to the previous stage, stage 3 offers more tools and technologies that facilitate working from anywhere and from any device. With the right tools and technologies in place, employees can work efficiently and effectively from anywhere, reducing the need for face-to-face meetings and improving collaboration. Shared document technologies and other collaboration tools, such as hybrid whiteboarding tools, can make it easier for employees to communicate and collaborate with each other, regardless of location, improving teamwork and problem solving. With the ability to work from anywhere, employees can have greater control

over their work–life balance and can be more flexible in their schedules, which can improve well-being and job satisfaction. However, in
this stage, employees are still expected to work mainly during the set
office hours, and the tools and technologies do not support asynchronous work, which they do in the next stage.

Stage 4: Asynchronous Work Culture

Before the COVID-19 pandemic, asynchronous collaboration more
often occurred between international teams than between local in-office
teams; with the pandemic, asynchronous work gained more attention.
Asynchronous work happens when employees do not work at the same
time, and this can bring a number of benefits to an organization and its
employees. With the ability to work anywhere and anytime, employees
can more effectively manage their time and prioritize their workload,
leading to improved productivity and decreased stress. Employees can
work at a time that best suits them, allowing for a better work–life balance and reducing the pressure of having to be available during specific
hours. By allowing employees to work when they are most productive and
motivated, asynchronous work can improve the quality and efficiency of
work done. Asynchronous work can be challenging, and it requires a
good strategy to facilitate collaboration and teamwork. There are several
strategies that can help to facilitate collaboration:

- Setting clear goals and deadlines and communicating them
  effectively. It is important to establish clear objectives and
  deadlines for each task, so that employees know what needs
  to be achieved by when. Project management tools can be of
  help to keep track of each team member's progress. Everyone
  involved in a project should know what is expected of them
  and by when. Communicating with stakeholders about
  progress and providing constant feedback are also important
  parts of a communication strategy.
- Employing time management techniques to break up work
  into manageable chunks to reduce stress and uncertainty
  when collaborating asynchronously.

- Democratizing knowledge through allowing team members to access all documents through a shared drive or SharePoint when documents are still in progress and not only once they are finalized.

When employees are working together on projects and share information and feedback at their own pace and time, the ways that they share the information and collaborate need to be beneficial for both the team and the employee. Therefore, agreeing upon the strategies upfront to facilitate optimal collaboration and teamwork is very important when working asynchronously.

Stage 5: Personalized Hybrid Work

In the last stage, employees are able to work anywhere and anytime, and technologies are in place to offer a true personalized hybrid employee experience. In order to fully realize these benefits, it is important that organizations invest in the right tools and technologies to support hybrid work. These may include cloud-based collaboration tools, virtual meeting software, and productivity apps, as well as tools for security and data management. With the right tools and technologies in place, organizations and employees can be more productive, efficient, and flexible, and they can take full advantage of the benefits of hybrid work. Ultimately, the goal is for employees and employers to be on the same page, by finding a unique solution that is not one-size-fits-all.

The difficulty lies in the fact that there is not one true hybrid strategy with processes and supporting tools that an organization can simply replicate and implement. There are guidelines, and some organizations are in late phases of experimentation to determine what does and does not work. There is also research that provides increasingly more insights and benchmarks. However, the culture and leadership of every organization are unique, and this uniqueness also brings a challenge. A hybrid strategy that works for one company might not work for another organization that is similar in terms of industry and size. Even within an organization, a hybrid strategy is not one-size-fits-all. For example, a team that often collaborates might require a different hybrid strategy than a team that mainly works with clients or on individual projects.

Overall, the leadership sets the tone. For example, CEOs who demand that all of their employees work at least 40 hours in office create a different tone than do leaders who work from home most of the time and who offer more or full flexibility to their employees. According to the Microsoft Work Trend Index,[4] 54 percent of people managers say that their company is out of touch with its employees. This is a huge challenge in coordinating the needs of the individuals, the needs of the team, and the needs of the organization. It can be even harder to stay in touch with employees who are remote, and keeping them engaged requires different processes than have existed in the past. *Harvard Business Review* concludes that an organized hybrid workplace is both effective and productive for both employees and employers, especially when considering how work is carried out.[5]

Creating a Tailored Hybrid Strategy

When strategizing for stage 5 (personalized hybrid work), different individuals or groups of individuals have different values, and needs within the organization could vary from the need for work flexibility (e.g., due to childcare responsibilities) to the desire to work as a digital nomad. Furthermore, on a smaller level, individuals who have a crowded house might want to go to the office to be able to focus on their work, whereas others who live alone go to the office to collaborate. The same situation applies to teams; an outside sales team that spends the majority of its time with customers, an engineering team that collaborates to design products, and a financial team that works with strictly confidential information all work toward an organization's goals, but their working styles differ.

It is important to take these differing perspectives into account when planning for hybrid work. A personalized and optimal employee experience needs to work for the individual, the team, and the organization. This means that we cannot settle for one-size-fits-all anymore, which makes it difficult to find the right solution. In my view, experimentation and adjustment must take place before solutions are found that work for all parties. However, in order to be effective, we need to look for a win–win–win situation. When working from home, some employees experience more autonomy, expect more privileges, and do not want to go back. Conversely, other team members experience sub-optimal situations in a hybrid or remote working environment, such as being alone in the office or having difficulties reaching a colleague. Response times are sometimes longer when employees and teams do not agree on a hybrid strategy. On the other hand, organizations are experiencing the situation where the demand for people to return to working in-house has not been well received. Many of the processes and agreements between organizations, teams, and individual employees are bound to culture and leadership behavior, but technology can help in creating a more personalized employee experience while still respecting team values and organizational boundaries. Figure 2.3 illustrates where technologies can help an entire organization and where different technologies might be needed to help in creating a more personalized employee experience.

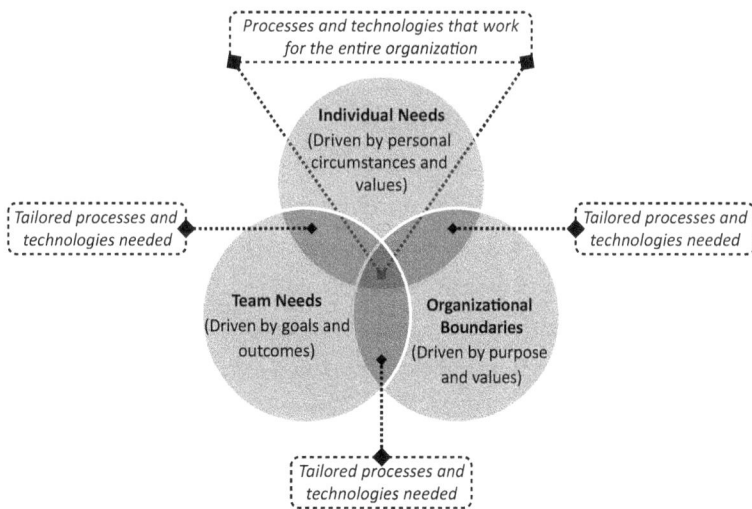

Figure 2.3 Framework for assessing technology needs for hybrid work

Individual Needs

All individuals experience work differently. Even in the same role, on the same team, and at the same company, different employees' own beliefs, values, and interpretations of their roles result in different degrees of performance, and their own unique experiences also require different needs for processes and techniques. Examples of individuals' needs include:

- *Flexible working or asynchronous working*: working when it best suits an individual
- *Remote working*: working from any location
- *Collaboration*: collaborating regardless of where an individual or their colleagues are
- *Sense of belonging*: needing to feel part of the team and the organization
- *Focus work*: needing to be able to focus for a certain period to get work done, without notifications and other pop-ups or distractions

Team Needs

Every team also has different needs. Some teams consist of individuals who each perform their tasks autonomously, whereas other teams consist of individuals who need daily meetings before they can move forward with their own tasks. This means that the approaches and technologies needed for each team vary, and therefore I advocate to look at team levels and not only at organizational levels. A Workgheist study[6] shows that 43 percent of workers feel that they spend too much time switching between digital tools, yet an analysis by Gartner predicts that "by 2024, in-person meetings will drop from 60 percent of enterprise meetings to 25 percent," necessitating the use of even more digital collaboration tools.[7]

Examples of teams' needs include the following:

- *Flexible working or asynchronous working*: having the ability to know when and how to reach other team members and tracking where people are in their contributions to the team's goals, for example, with an objective key result (OKR) tracking app.
- *Remote working*: agreeing on when team members are online and knowing who is in which office and when, which can very easily be achieved with apps, even for free.
- *Collaboration*: not only showing a final product or deliverable, but also showing work in progress in real time by utilizing

collaboration apps, where multiple people can access documents in real time, and technologies, such as Microsoft's Viva platform, that leverage machine learning to categorize topics that employees are working on. This helps in identifying who in the same organization is working on the same topic, which is very helpful in decentralized multinationals. Such apps can help in preventing employees from reinventing the wheel and can facilitate in harnessing collective knowledge for the organization regardless of team members' work locations.

- *Sense of belonging*: the feeling of being accepted and valued as a member of a team or an organization. A sense of belonging is important for every team to allow each member to contribute to their best ability. Colocated teams, especially those across different time zones, became more inclusive during the COVID-19 pandemic, whereas, beforehand, when in-office, spontaneous meetings happened, people who were not in the office missed out entirely (such meetings were rarely recorded). When everyone was working from home, all team members, regardless of whether they were a remote employee or located in office, were in the same situation. A link to a virtual meeting was included in a meeting invite, and meetings were recorded for people to view at their own convenience. Teams also learned that constantly reviewing recordings can be exhausting, and many teams improved their meeting note-taking by tagging people to action items. Upcoming AI solutions could take these manual tasks away. They offer hybrid teams better summarized meeting notes and insights in how inclusive their meetings are.

Organizational Boundaries

Over the last few years, more organizations have been embracing and planning to facilitate hybrid work but not to the extent that employees want it to be done. How strong an organization's position is on the labor market can influence decisions on to what extent employees' hybrid work needs should be part of the organization's talent retention strategy.

Organizations that want employees to come more often into the office are struggling to do so, and organizations are not successful in creating a good enough reason for employees to want to work in the office. Different people have different needs, and these can also vary within employee life cycles.

Organizations also question if remote workers are still working on the priorities of the company and driving the right amount of impact. Organizations struggle to understand how their employees are feeling and if they still contribute to the (shifted) priorities. Organizations do not always understand how to make employees aware that priorities have shifted or how to make sure that employees adjust their focus. Before the COVID-19 pandemic, difficult conversations, performance reviews, and restructuring conversations happened in person, and after a tough conversation, employees could vent to their colleagues and then move forward. In 2021, I participated in a Mapiq Talks webinar together with Tim Oldman, founder and CEO of Leesman,* and he mentioned a customer of his that has employees who operate a contact center for emergency services. He mentioned that those agents need to decompress after each call by talking to another human being who understands what they do because they have had similar experiences. Even when technology makes it possible to perform such jobs from home, the human aspect is important.

In the tension between the value of physical and virtual interactions, organizations often find it difficult to ensure an optimal experience for everyone and often opt for a hybrid solution as a middling, suboptimal compromise. We have all been in a Zoom or Teams meeting where the experience was suboptimal. Most of the interviews for this book were conducted remotely. During one interview, there was roadwork being done near my location, and the Internet was inaccessible for 15 minutes. Another time, the video kept freezing and the application completely shut down. These are all scenarios that employees experience on a weekly or sometimes even daily basis that make remote work difficult. Sometimes being physically together actually is the better

---

* Leesman measures and analyzes employee workplace experiences for individual organizations, giving them the data and insights necessary to create outstanding work environments.

option. If being physically together is not an option, there are many technologies available or being developed that can help in creating a more optimal candidate and employee experience in the hybrid world. Looking for an optimal solution creates a more inclusive workspace, and technologies can help employers in not only accommodate for the majority of voices but also actually make the world of work more inclusive for everyone.

Human capital management (HCM) software is critical for any modern organization and even more so in a hybrid world. In general, HCM software includes core HR, talent management, workforce management, and service delivery tools and can include other technologies including analytic tools. Cloud-based HCM is key to hybrid workplace technology; allowing all systems to be available remotely ensures that data is accessible and maintained by employees, managers, and HR regardless of from where and when the employees access the systems. These tools and technologies can be implemented throughout the entire employee life cycle, and examples include the following:

- *Flexible working*: Employees felt the need to be always available online during the pandemic to "compensate" for not being visible enough. This resulted in high levels of stress for many. Leveraging technologies that automatically only send e-mails when the recipient is working can reduce such stress and facilitate asynchronous work.
- *Remote working*: While some employees dream of working from the beach for a few weeks or months, not every organization has the technology to facilitate such an arrangement. Employees in the office have easier and faster access to information, thanks to having better access to technology and infrastructure to support their work at the office. Slow Internet connections and the inability to access certain resources from home make it difficult to be in the know and demonstrate competence. Further, device and software security issues can be harmful to both the employee and the employer. For example, not all data is allowed to be accessed from outside the EU.

- *Collaboration*: Fostering collaboration can be harder in a hybrid work situation. Organizational network analysis (ONA) can help with hybrid planning for hybrid work, by providing a clear understanding of how work is currently done within an organization. I share more in Chapter 5 on how ONA can help.
- *Sense of belonging*: Though technologies are improving, being physically distanced all the time can make employees less engaged and reduce their sense of belonging. Virtual cocktail hours do not replace the need to physically interact. Though various virtual tools have become available, they do not satisfy the need for the sense of belonging. Leveraging ONA could also help in identifying who is isolated within an organization and how to foster a better sense of belonging.

When setting these processes and implementing technologies for hybrid work, it is very important to consider how to be as inclusive as possible for every individual in the team. The pandemic brought many issues to the surface but also created an opportunity to be more inclusive to all individuals. Tools, such as sign language, captioning and transcribing of all-hands meetings, webinars, and other events, are easy to implement, instantly make information available to more employees, and are inclusive. In Chapter 4, I share in more detail how technology can help in creating a more inclusive employee experience.

Tools and Technologies Through the Employee Life Cycle That Support Hybrid Work

There are many tools and technologies available that can support a hybrid work strategy throughout the employee life cycle, and many more will be made available in the future. When creating a hybrid work strategy and its supporting software, it is important to understand what makes employees better at their jobs and what makes them feel better. In addition, the hybrid work strategy needs to align with the organization's overall strategy. This coordination makes establishing a hybrid work strategy and finding the right complementary technology truly complex.

I do recommend setting hypotheses and experimenting with what works for every part of the employee life cycle, which can be a systematic and iterative process. Figure 2.4 shows the process for setting hypotheses and conducting experiments to find the right technology for every part of the employee life cycle.

Identifying the various stages of the employee life cycle in the organization and prioritizing at what stage the experiment will be conducted is the first step. Performing a comprehensive analysis of the organization's needs and pain points at each stage of the employee life cycle is second. It is important to engage with different stakeholders, such as HR professionals, leaders, and employees themselves, to gain insights into the challenges and areas for improvement. Based on the needs analysis, a specific hypothesis that can address the identified challenges needs to be

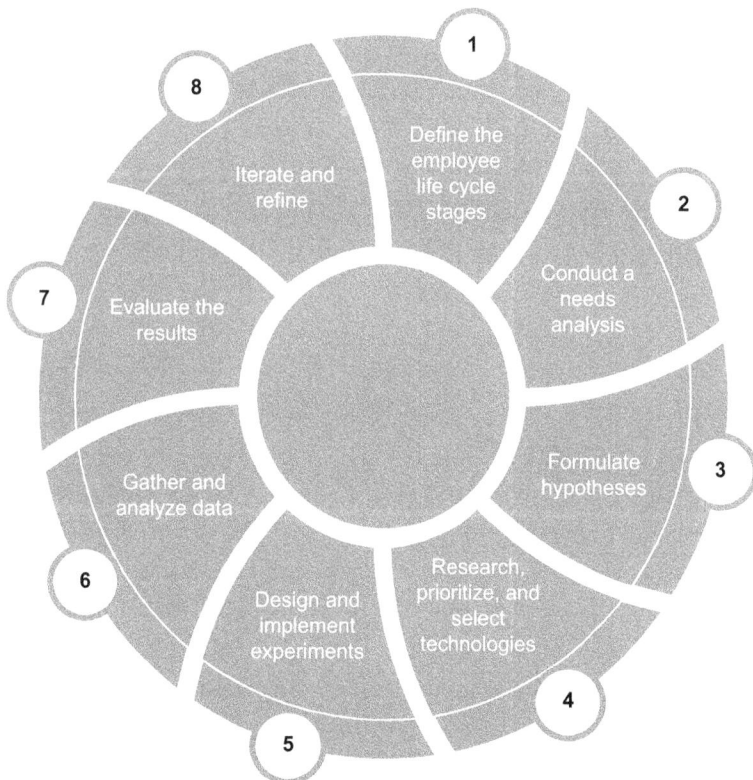

Figure 2.4 Process for setting hypotheses and conducting experiments for finding the right technology for every part of the employee life cycle

formulated. An example of a hypothesis for the onboarding process could be "implementing a mobile-based onboarding platform will improve the effectiveness of the onboarding process." Once the hypothesis is set, it is important to explore the market to identify technologies and solutions that align with it. Engaging with different technology vendors can, for example, be done through attending industry conferences, reading case studies, and seeking recommendations from peers. Based on their features, capabilities, scalability, integration options, costs, and alignment with the organization's specific needs, the technologies need to be evaluated. Third parties can be of help in the vendor selection process and in prioritizing the technologies that have the highest potential to effectively address the identified challenges.

It is important to test the selected technologies through experiments before implementing and scaling them across the organization. The success criteria of the experiment need to be clear upfront, and the objectives and metrics need to align with the hypotheses. For example, if the hypothesis is to improve the onboarding process, metrics could include time to productivity, employee satisfaction scores, and manager feedback. When implementing the experiments, it is important to deploy the selected technologies in a controlled environment or with a specific group of employees and to ensure that experiments are well documented and any necessary training or support is provided to the participants.

Organizations should collect relevant data and feedback throughout the experiment's duration, monitor the identified metrics, and capture qualitative insights through surveys, interviews, or focus groups. It is important to analyze the data to determine the impact of the technologies on the employee life cycle stages. At the end of the experiment, the outcomes should be assessed against the initial hypotheses. The data needs to be analyzed to identify strengths, weaknesses, and areas for improvement. It is crucial to determine whether the technologies have achieved the desired outcomes and whether they can be scaled, if they require further iterations or need to be sunsetted. Based on the evaluation's results, the approach can be iterated or refined. Sometimes, however, the experiment shows that it is not the right technology to reach the intended results. Organizations then should decide to sunset the chosen technology and start a new experiment or replace the technologies as needed to address any shortcomings or maximize the effectiveness. It is important to repeat the experimentation process to continuously optimize technology solutions across the employee life cycle.

Experimentation is an ongoing process, and it is crucial to involve stakeholders, gather feedback, and stay updated on emerging technologies to ensure that the organization's technology landscape evolves with the changing needs of the employee life cycle.

Needed to support a hybrid work strategy are communication and collaboration tools and platforms, project management tools, virtual collaboration tools, productivity tools (such as OKR tools or time tracking), employee engagement and feedback technologies, and foundational IT support and security tools. Even the types of platforms can vary depending on intent. For example, a video interview for hiring might require a particular level of security in software, whereas different features might be needed for a virtual coffee meeting where colleagues informally discuss the continuation of a project. Figure 2.5 is a visualization of the tools and technologies that could be part of an organization's hybrid strategy, and later I elaborate on the technologies that are implemented at each stage of the life cycle.

Brand and Recruit

Hybrid recruitment is a mix of virtual recruitment tactics and physical in-person recruiting. This combination leverages the top possibilities of both talent acquisition strategies as one, with the purpose of driving an even better outcome than each of these strategies individually could. The COVID-19 pandemic allowed us to brand and recruit fully in the virtual world, and this has created new and finetuned technologies to better serve both organizations and candidates.

When attracting new employees, I believe that it is important to be transparent when discussing what the hiring organization's motivation and plan are for implementing a hybrid strategy. The reality is that many organizations communicate a motivation but do not share a plan for achieving it. A disconnect with what the new hire expects in terms of hybrid working and what the employer actually offers can cause people to quit in the first few weeks of their employment. Employer branding was

Brand and Recruit	Onboard and Ramp Up	Learn and Develop	Engage and Retain	Offboard and Rehire
• Vacancy video technology • Video interviewing technology • Automated screening apps • Pre-employment tests and online assessments • Voice and personality analysis, AI tools	• Cloud-based onboarding applications • Buddy matching technology • Virtual coffee apps • Organizational network analysis (ONA)	• Coaching apps • Online learning platforms • Mixed reality learning platforms • Learning management system • Learning experience platform	• Collaboration platforms • Video conferencing software • Mobile security software • Objective key result apps • Desk reservation systems • Project management software	• Communication tools • Remote security technologies • Knowledge capturing tools • Social media

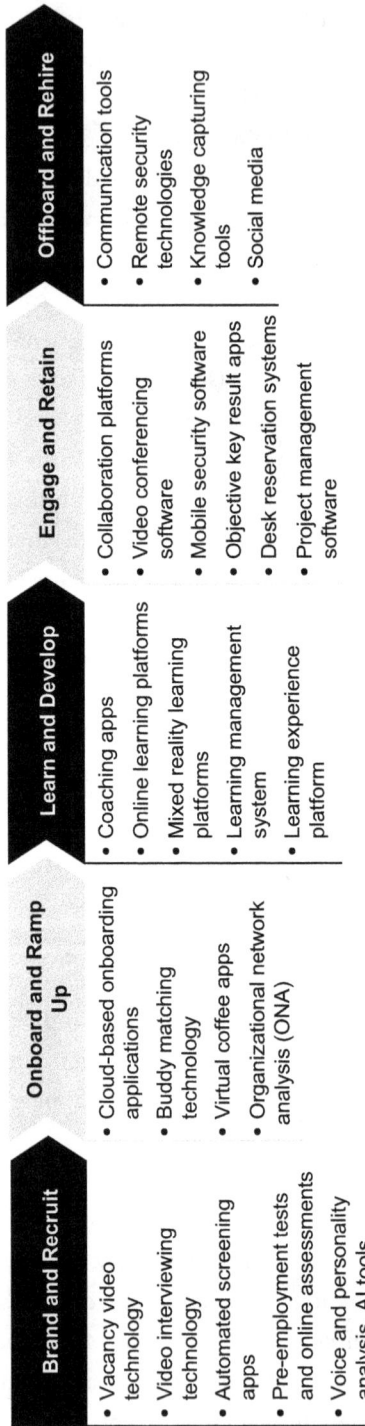

Figure 2.5 Technologies to support hybrid work throughout the employee life cycle

already mainly done online, but now it is also adding new technologies to the mix to increase engagement. Organizations are, for example, offering videos about vacancies and in Chapter 6, I share more on how the metaverse can contribute to hybrid employer branding.

Some tools offer possibilities sifting through many resumes to find the most suitable candidate, whereas others, such as Cammio,[†] have additional functionalities that allow recruiters to create a video about a vacancy to create higher engagement with candidates. For example, they allow organizations to evaluate the candidate's experience with the skills you are looking for, even if they are not explicitly mentioned in their CV. The video interview is not an alternative to an in-person interview, but it can be used as a filter to bring only the very best candidates to an interview. When talent is scarce, organizations are looking for the same talent, and some talents can even work across industries, it makes sense that organizations want to stand out and are leveraging video to show more of their employer brand. When I interviewed Sandhna Chintoe, International Managing Director of Cammio, she mentioned that they noticed a shift in that organizations focus more on using Cammio for branding purposes, whereas before the Great Resignation, the focus was on using it for selection purposes.

Candidate Screening, Interviews, and Assessments

Hiring is very costly for an organization, because when hiring, managers and their directs spend time interviewing and are not contributing to their daily operations. Video interviewing tools allow HR teams the flexibility and accessibility to reach talent located around the world and can be great resource-saving alternatives to traditional interviews. One of the biggest complaints made by recruitment teams is "no-show" interviews, which waste valuable time. As a result, more organizations are increasingly making use of automatic candidate screening applications, online assessments, and automatic or video interviewing tools. Many organizations are combining virtual and physical screenings.

[†] Cammio was founded to add personality to resumes, and it connects candidates and employers with video. More on https://cammio.com/about-cammio.

While Zoom, Google Hangout, Teams, or similar programs are being used for interviews as a replacement for the in-person interview, more technologies are becoming available that offer a more optimal candidate experience. There are different offerings available, and as an organization, you can choose to conduct your interviews live or allow them to happen asynchronously by recording the questions for each candidate. Some platforms offer a variety of options, such as asynchronous interviewing, one-way interviewing, and live interviewing, while others offer only one. Some of these tools even have the option to directly integrate with an applicant tracking system (ATS), which could be an advantage for some organizations. Moreover, where some of them allow candidates to rerecord their messages, others do not allow candidates to stop, pause, redo, or review. These differences make it important to decide what would work the best for different teams within an organization before deciding to land on one tool. Especially relevant if you are operating in multiple countries and you want to support local-language interviews is that technologies that use AI do not always support local languages, meaning that the local experience can be suboptimal.

Live interviews can of course be done with almost any video conferencing tool, but one thing that Sandhna pointed out was compliance. Cammio's software requires candidates to consent with the recording, and if the candidate does not consent, then the software prevents the recruiter or hiring manager from recording. In addition, all of the data from their platform is stored in the EU. Both of these points can be very important if you are a European-based or operated organization.

Further, there are tools, apps, and platforms that help organizations with their pre-employment tests, assessments, and skills, competency, and talent matching. All are AI enabled and can be easily used anywhere in the world. Various AI tools, such as voice and personality analysis, can be applied. These capture and store transcripts as well as interviewer scores and comments all in one place for future reviews.

Recruiters, managers, candidates, interviewers, and approvers need the ability to perform all their actions remotely, and the ATS should allow for this. Another consideration is the breadth and depth of the organization's talent pool. With a hybrid workforce, organizations are no longer confined to hiring employees within a specific city, state, or country. Organizations may want to update their recruiting strategy to determine how best to take advantage of this new opportunity.

Onboard and Ramp Up

Hybrid onboarding refers to the process of integrating new employees into a company's culture, systems, and processes through a combination of in-person and remote activities. Before the COVID-19 pandemic, onboarding, or the lack thereof, already led people to leave their jobs within the first few months. A strong onboarding process is correlated with better performance and improved employee engagement.[8]

Before the pandemic, onboarding usually took place in the physical office, and sometimes employees were even flown to particular locations to train. With the rise of remote work, hybrid onboarding has become increasingly popular as it allows organizations to provide a comprehensive onboarding experience for new hires, regardless of their physical location. With the potential for new employees to be in 100 percent remote positions, organizations need to rethink their approach to onboarding and may need a cloud-based onboarding application that provides flexibility and security. These tools provide a location-independent way to introduce new employees to their teams. It is important to include an introduction to the company culture as well. The risk of 100 percent remote onboarding can be that the onboarding tools and applications only focus on sharing information such as policies, training materials, and generic information about organizations.

When organizations hire and onboard their employees entirely remotely, it is harder to ensure that the employees are building social capital. Gaining social capital is crucial for thriving in an organization. Building relationship currency is hard when entering a new organization. A manager normally opens their network, but in a hybrid world this needs to be done more purposefully. Tools for virtual buddy matching and virtual coffees, where you are randomly matched to drink a coffee with another person in the organization, could be helpful. Using ONA can also give the organization an indication that employees are also well connected outside of their daily organizations. Though these tools do help, I personally think a hybrid onboarding option is still the best for building social capital. Where learning about an organization's processes and many other trainings can be done online and thus remotely, a real, deep relationship building still happens on a human level, for me that still means occasionally in-person enjoying a coffee or meal together.

Learn and Develop

Hybrid learning and development is an approach to training and education that combines traditional classroom-based learning with digital and remote learning technologies. This model offers a blended learning experience that combines the benefits of face-to-face instruction with the flexibility and accessibility of online learning. This model has become increasingly popular in the wake of the COVID-19 pandemic, as it offers a safe and convenient way for organizations to provide ongoing training and development to their employees, regardless of their physical location.

A coaching leadership style requires leaders and managers not needing to know everything in order to be effective; instead, they know how to empower their direct reports. Whereas in the past, managers could see how and what everyone was doing and could adjust their management style accordingly, remote and hybrid working arrangements require a different style. For example, within the hybrid and remote world of work, employees are more in need of a coaching manager, and both managers and employees need to learn how to adjust to this new style. Employees can also look beyond their manager for coaching, mentoring, and sponsoring. Many employees are struggling with visibility, which leads to the "always on" culture, where employees feel the need to always be available to make themselves visible and prove that they are productive. In my view, it is better when employees receive help from their own managers or mentors in building a larger network on their own manager and skip-level manager levels. In the changing world of work, I see more employees asking for a sponsor to advocate on their behalf during calibration and more mentors from within the company to facilitate their development.

Before the pandemic, the online learning industry was already growing, and the industry is projected to grow at an average of 11 percent annually, reaching a value of over USD37 billion by 2026.[9] Online learning platforms have become more popular for employees, and during the pandemic, people went beyond learning required and provided by their employers. Platforms such as Coursera went from having 44 million users in 2019 to 92 million users in 2021, because of the increase in online learning demands.[10]

Cultivating workers' skills through learning applications is key for any organization today, including those with hybrid workplaces. To create an optimal employee experience and meet compliance needs, training needs to be adjusted to work optimally in a hybrid workplace. Especially if part of the employees are colocated and part are 100 percent remote, each group might require a different learning path and different tools to support training. Learning management systems (LMS) and learning experience platforms (LXP) can facilitate training from anywhere at any time, but additional investments in technologies should be considered to support hybrid workplaces for a better employee experience. Working hybrid requires employees to work more digitally and, regardless of the role (finance, HR, administration, and IT), this situation requires different skills, including remote work and digital skills. Working hybrid also requires different management and leadership techniques, and coaching platforms are quickly responding to this demand. In Chapter 1, I shared more on the new skills required of leadership and the effect of hybrid work on different skills needed.

Engage and Retain

Engaging and retaining employees in a hybrid work model refers to the strategies and actions that organizations can take to maintain high levels of employee satisfaction, motivation, and commitment in a work environment that combines remote and in-person work. This involves creating an inclusive and supportive workplace culture that values and respects the needs and preferences of all employees, regardless of their physical location. I keep on stressing that different groups within an organization have different needs. These make a one-size-fits-all strategy a risk in terms of losing top talent to other organizations that are better at facilitating a more personalized employee experience that will help these individuals thrive. Senior leaders already have their networks and have built strong social capital over the course of their careers. They can continue to hold these strong relations remotely, and more often their organizations need them to share their knowledge and networks. However, early in their careers, individuals need to build social capital, create strong relations, and learn from more experienced employees in their organizations. Another difference is that leaders oftentimes have an appropriate home office to allow them to work from home, whereas junior employees sometimes cohabit spaces and have no access to an individual office at home. Some of these issues are related to organizational culture and cannot be solved with technology. Creating a culture and discipline to democratize knowledge within an organization and leveraging collaboration and communication tools to make sure that hybrid employees are as involved as those in the office will contribute to better access to knowledge and employees being able to do their jobs well.

Communication and Collaboration Platforms

Collaboration in hybrid work refers to the process of working together and sharing ideas, resources, and information in a mixed-location work environment, where some team members work remotely while others work in a physical office. In a hybrid work model, it is important for team members to have effective communication and collaboration tools and processes in place to ensure that everyone can work together effectively regardless of location.

A few tips for achieving effective collaboration in a hybrid work environment are illustrated in Figure 2.6 and the example technologies will be explained in the next paragraphs.

Video Conferencing Software

During the pandemic, the use of video conferencing software grew exponentially. Organizations quickly expanded the use of conferencing software, and it is not possible to imagine transitioning into a hybrid working model without using such software. Video conferencing platforms will be crucial in enabling remote and in-office team members to connect. They are more personal and engaging than a phone call, and they are much more effective and sustainable than commuting to the office. Different vendors are offering different features to offer optimal hybrid workplace experiences. One of the key features that they are working on is

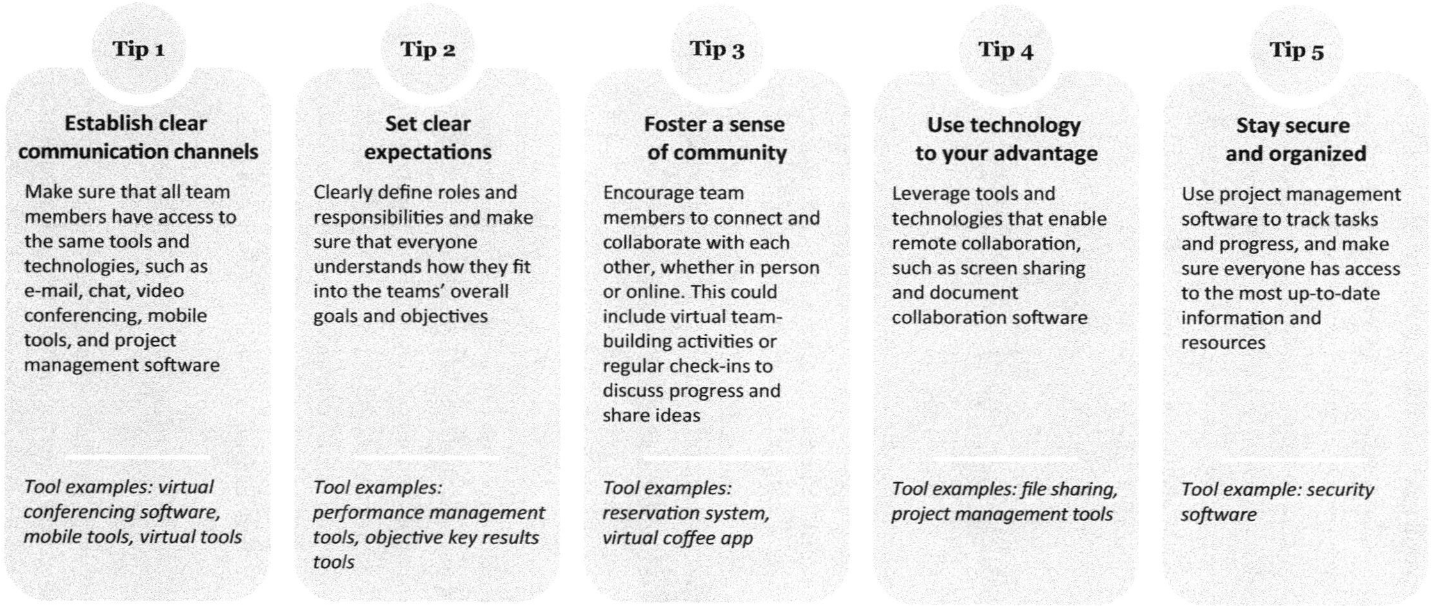

Tip 1

Establish clear communication channels

Make sure that all team members have access to the same tools and technologies, such as e-mail, chat, video conferencing, mobile tools, and project management software

Tool examples: virtual conferencing software, mobile tools, virtual tools

Tip 2

Set clear expectations

Clearly define roles and responsibilities and make sure that everyone understands how they fit into the teams' overall goals and objectives

Tool examples: performance management tools, objective key results tools

Tip 3

Foster a sense of community

Encourage team members to connect and collaborate with each other, whether in person or online. This could include virtual team-building activities or regular check-ins to discuss progress and share ideas

Tool examples: reservation system, virtual coffee app

Tip 4

Use technology to your advantage

Leverage tools and technologies that enable remote collaboration, such as screen sharing and document collaboration software

Tool examples: file sharing, project management tools

Tip 5

Stay secure and organized

Use project management software to track tasks and progress, and make sure everyone has access to the most up-to-date information and resources

Tool example: security software

Figure 2.6 Tips for achieving effective collaboration in a hybrid working environment

individual hybrid framing. This feature treats meeting participants equally and is meant to help employees to better understand the body language and facial expressions of other employees. All known platforms offer great video conferencing software, but some also offer additional features that can be worth considering. For example, collaboration tools, such as file sharing and messaging, make it easier to follow up with colleagues after a meeting. Additionally, speech-to-text real-time captioning, AI recap, and automatic summary are ideal for hearing-impaired employees and non-native speakers.

Mobile Tools

Even before the COVID-19 pandemic, mobile use was growing exponentially. When the pandemic hit, mobile tools became lifelines for keeping workers connected, executing technology implementation, and pivoting to a new normal. Whether employees are working in office or working remotely on a particular day, they need certain capabilities for getting their work done. These include connectivity, the ability to look up organization information, and the ability to provide approvals. Mobile software and tools are key to ensuring this productivity.

Virtual Tools

The overload on video calls can result in feelings of tiredness, anxiousness, and sometimes even burnout or depression. This phenomenon is known as "Zoom fatigue," and it was integral in driving the design of alternative virtual collaboration tools and in popularizing whiteboarding. These apps help teams with real-time or asynchronous brainstorming and collaboration. Sharing ideas and drawing them on a board together is much less monotonous than listening to everyone talk all the time.

Performance Management Tools

In an environment where the employee–manager relationship is remote or only occasionally in-person, employees need clear goals and regular check-ins to ensure they are receiving timely feedback. Managers can easily get into the "out of sight, out of mind" mentality, leaving the employee on their own and unsure if their performance is meeting expectations. Technology is critical in supporting this aspect of the hybrid workplace, but continuous performance management is the first strategic approach. Such management involves top leadership and HR teams having clear messaging around best practices and methodologies to support managers' training in giving feedback. OKR tools, such as Viva Goals, connect the tasks and objectives of different teams to the strategic priorities of an organization and help measure the progress of both individuals and teams.

Reservation System

Employees need a way to reserve their workspaces when organizations plan to offer hot desking or hoteling. It may be possible to utilize the same application that is used for booking meeting rooms. However, if numerous hoteling options are offered, a more targeted or intuitive application to facilitate the reservation process is preferred. More advanced technologies offer office neighborhoods, which are a way to organize the workplace so that people who need to collaborate or who have similar workspace needs sit together in one area.

Virtual Coffee Apps

Remote work can be isolating for employees and reduces the opportunity to meet other employees and build a network across teams, departments, and different lines of hierarchy. Virtual coffee apps give employees the opportunity to build social capital by meeting different employees outside of their regular group and to build cross-functional connections. These virtual breaks can give employees a pause from their routine and spark innovation while also building a wider network. Collaboration tools such as Microsoft Teams and Slack offer various apps to facilitate these randomized coffees.

File Sharing

All day, knowledge workers are working on files, from documents to videos to even software. File-sharing tools enable teams to quickly distribute and transfer files and provide access to other members. These applications remove the transfer process from e-mail and instant messaging tools, relieving inboxes from the distracting flood of files and notifications. With a document management system in place, you can control who within your organization can see, edit, and delete files. To ensure that all employees have the same access to the information they require, there may be a need to digitize existing files, including those that continue to require a wet signature, such as documents for government agencies. Microsoft and Google both offer this in their suite, but Box and Citrix ShareFile are also popular options. When choosing such a tool, it is important that they communicate or integrate with your other collaboration tools. This helps employees to track, manage, and connect on projects.

Project Management

When collaborating with multiple teams across multiple locations, platforms such as Trello and Asana can help your employees to coordinate and keep track of their tasks and budgets. This again helps to stay connected even when employees work asynchronously.

Security Software

Flexible work environments require a sophisticated approach to security. Many organizations have relied on VPNs, but some security experts believe these leave organizations vulnerable to bad actors, since in many cases, VPN authentication gives a user unfettered access to the corporate network. In response, many organizations are looking at alternative remote access methods, such as zero-trust network access.

Developments on communication and collaboration technologies are occurring rapidly, and most of us are still experimenting and finding more optimal ways to operate in this hybrid world. Actively monitoring through listening systems to learn what is and is not working can help organizations to improve their hybrid strategy in the coming years. Transparent communication also plays a crucial role in developing and maintaining trust with employees. When experiments are happening or decisions are not transparent, communication can really help employees to stay committed. In general, integrations of technologies are key for reducing app overload and keeping context switching for your employees to a minimum.

Lastly, keeping the culture and values top of mind and embraced by everyone regardless of location can be a hard task. It can be hard for organizations to ensure that employees commit to and experience a common set of values when working in a hybrid world. It is important to be transparent about how people are contributing to and how they fit in with the common goals of the organization. As Theresa Sigillito Hollema writes in her book *Virtual Teams Across Cultures*:

> *successful global virtual teams need culturally competent people to realize the potential the diversity of thought and experience in the team offers. Developing cultural competence includes learning through social research and books, conversations with other colleagues and experiences that push one's personal boundaries.*

She also mentions that it is possible to develop cultural competence virtually, and virtual team members benefit when teams intentionally dedicate time and energy toward that endeavor.[11]

By following these tips, teams can effectively collaborate in a hybrid work environment and achieve their goals, even when team members are not all working from the same location.

Offboard and Rehire

Offboarding employees with hybrid technologies refers to the process of transitioning employees out of an organization while leveraging a combination of traditional and digital tools and systems. When offboarding fully remote or in a hybrid capacity, it is important to communicate clearly with the employees and inform them properly about what is expected and how they can securely return their devices. Security is key and can be ensured by already deactivating badges and blocking laptops before they are sent by the employee. Knowledge transfer is also very important. When employees who are working partly or 100 percent remotely leave, it is key to ensure that the departing employees' knowledge and responsibilities are transferred to other team members or departments. Therefore, it is important that knowledge is captured during the employee's employment in the proper systems so it can easily be transferred. Finally, stay in touch with former employees and potentially reach out to alumni who left because a hybrid work arrangement had not been an option in the past. The labor market is tight, and talent is scarce, so whenever organizations have a great hire and a cultural fit, they need to solidify those relationships. Whereas, in the past, some companies organized in-person alumni events, some applications and a good hybrid alumni strategy should help organizations to keep an eye out for those talents and win them back.

The Impact of Hybrid Work for Frontline Workers

The impact of hybrid work on frontline workers will depend on a variety of factors. Similar to the information workers strategy on individual needs, the specific needs of the role of a frontline worker, the values of their team, and organizational boundaries can also be applied for the frontline employees. Organizations with both frontline and information workers cannot miss frontline workers when creating and communicating their hybrid work strategy. There can be a huge gap between both groups of employees, since hybrid is harder to implement and can most of the times only be implemented in a different way for frontline workers.

When setting and communicating this strategy, it is important to keep it in line with the organization's values and make sure that those are reflected in both the information workers and the frontline workers strategy. It is important for organizations to consider the unique needs and challenges of their frontline workforce and how in some countries labor laws and union agreements need to be considered when implementing a hybrid strategy. With that said, some potential impacts for frontline workers can include more flexibility and enhanced collaboration. Challenges with implementing more and new technology with frontline workers are also present and include the need to adapt to new technology and tools and the potential for technical issues to arise and disrupt work.

Case: A Hybrid Work Strategy

I interviewed Senior HR Director of Cognizant‡ Ido Shikma about his company's hybrid strategy. At Cognizant, the organization went through a few steps to optimize their hybrid model work. For Cognizant, the hybrid model is not new; even before the pandemic, employees only came to the office for specific reasons. To make the hybrid model work even better for both the organization and its employees, Cognizant continues to learn, experiment, and improve in different parts of the organization.

At Cognizant, they looked at how people want to work, in three phases:

1. *Phase 1*: How do we continue to take care of our people on an operational level (e.g., leasing home-office furniture) and on a personal level (e.g., to prevent isolation)?
2. *Phase 2*: (on a more individual level) How as an employee can I better manage and adjust my working style and really grow in self-management?
3. *Phase 3*: How do we ensure an optimal way of working, learning from both the time when employees were fully remote and the stage when employees returned to work?

"It is important to continue the emotional connection and keep employees intrinsically motivated and engaged to enable a willingness to come to the office. In the office employees really connect," Ido explains. Therefore, it is important while facilitating optimal remote working to also find the optimal situations or events for

(Continues)

‡ Cognizant is an American multinational information technology services and consulting company that employs over 330,000 individuals across the globe. Cognizant's Digital Interactive Experience is recognized as having a strong vision for the future of experiences and its expertise to bring this vision to life.

(*Continued*)

employees to connect in the office. At Cognizant, they looked at three different levels for engagement in the office with employees:

1. *The organizational level*: connecting and engaging employees by organizing events, for example, a Diwali celebration, or by sending a token of appreciation to all associates. These collective initiatives might be experienced as a one-way engagement where the collective scope is leading.
2. *Team level*: connecting on a team level with either your functional or cross-functional team. This allows for more personal interaction and focus on unique teams and groups within the organization.
3. *Customer level*: connecting through customer events. Employees and clients interact and engage over specific themes.

Research at Cognizant shows that connections on a team level generate the most engagement and have a positive effect on retention. Cognizant is a large international organization, so connecting on the team level can be a challenge. That is why at Cognizant every person has both a business and a people manager. This was already the case in some form before the pandemic, but the focus has increased. These local managers do give input on performance but having someone locally that cares and connects you to the local organization has also had a positive effect on retention. Some managers are already great at creating engagement remotely, but for others the face-to-face component stays important, and having this locally available really adds to a positive employee experience. Analytics also contribute to inform managers on a team level about what they could do differently to help their teams feel and be better.

One of the things that I have heard from many of my customers is that it is hard to get employees to attend large company meetings and that if people do attend, they are multitasking or not very engaged. It is important to understand that when you need employees to show up, digitally in an all-hands meeting or physically in the office, you are claiming valuable time. If as an organization you require employees' attendance, make sure that it is valuable for those attending. After they reimagined their all-hands meetings at Cognizant, the attendance rate increased threefold.

What I find really interesting from Cognizant is that they realized that the one-size-fits-all approach was not working. They identified multiple groups within the organization and made tools, applications, and solutions available for these groups. The top-down approach has been reduced and the emphasis has been placed on the manager–employee relationship. Managers have operational empowerment to assess and understand the needs of the employees. Even two employees with the same title, responsibilities, and years of experience can have different needs. Operationally empowering managers to offer tools and applications based on employees' individual needs really comes close to achieving the individual employee experience in a hybrid world. As Ido shared,

> the essence of human resources is to make it personal. The creation of a personal connection between the individual employee and the organization is the most important. The context, the environment or the technology can change, but the essence won't.

Ido sees the future as providing more freedom and independence for both customers and employees. To create a work life that matches the life stage of the individual employee and allows for the work life to change overtime depends on the life stage that the individual is in. For organizations, three things will be important in the future:

1. Full remote and full in-office are the extremes on the spectrum. Most employees will be in need of some form of hybrid along this spectrum. Having the ability and technology in place to facilitate and adjust to the evolving journey of every individual will be crucial.
2. We will realize there is no replacement for human contact, so organizations need to facilitate this even when technology evolves.

(*Continues*)

(*Continued*)

3. The development toward a real personalized employee experience will continue, and organizations need to continue to invest in optimizing this.

Both the organization and the individual employee do carry the responsibility for safety and flexibility. The technology will continue to develop at a rapid pace, and investments are being made continuously. Next to the development of technology, we also need to continue to invest in the ability of self-management and the sense of ownership with all employees. To really teach and facilitate how to cope with these developments, how to take ownership of your own career, and how to make a personalized employee experience work for you as an individual needs more awareness and investment to make both the technology and the human development work hand in hand.

Conclusion

The hybrid way of working is forcing organizations to think differently about technologies, and the tools and technologies being offered are growing exponentially. Therefore, it is crucial to have a strategy in place before deciding on what technologies will enhance the employee experience. HR teams need to collaborate closely with IT organizations to prevent a one-size-fits-all purchase. HR teams can assess individuals' needs, teams' needs, and organizational boundaries, and accordingly, they can decide what the optimal technologies are to facilitate an optimal employee experience.

It can be a pitfall for organizations to invest in all kinds of technologies without having a long-term hybrid strategy in place. Organizations need to assess where they are on the five stages and create a roadmap toward the personalized hybrid strategy, while taking the individual privileges, the team values, and the organizational boundaries into account. After the strategy is set, different teams in the organization can experiment in finding the right technologies that fit the new hybrid strategy.

Starting with new technologies without understanding how these fit within the hybrid strategy can hold organizations back from reaching the intended results. Ultimately, the goal is for employees and employers to be on the same page, finding a unique solution that is not a one-size-fits-all.

Implementing a strategy for hybrid work is crucial throughout all aspects of the employee life cycle. A hybrid work strategy recognizes the unique needs and preferences of employees at different stages of their careers. From recruitment and onboarding to career development and offboarding, organizations must adapt. A hybrid work strategy promotes flexibility and work–life balance. Moreover, a hybrid work strategy enhances productivity and collaboration. By providing employees with the freedom to work in environments that suit their individual prefer-ences, such as remote or in-office settings, organizations can leverage the benefits of both approaches. Remote work often offers reduced distractions and increased focus, while in-person collaboration fosters creativity, spontaneous interactions, and team bonding. Combining these elements through a hybrid model allows employees to optimize their work environment for different tasks and achieve their best individual and team performance. By embracing flexibility, promoting work–life balance, enhancing productivity and collaboration, and contributing to the organization's success, a hybrid work strategy has become a vital element of the modern workplace.

CHAPTER 3

Employee Well-Being

We live in a society where the aim is to get as many people as possible to work for as long as possible and as much as possible. Employees increasingly have to balance their demanding jobs with familial responsibilities, pressure of societal norms, or personal aspirations. They are called upon to provide informal care for children, parents, or others, and at the same time, work full-time, and they must do all this for decades, until retirement. It is clear that quite a lot is being asked of our employees and that this great demand will not disappear.

In Microsoft's Work Trend Index, 47 percent of respondents reported that they are more likely to prioritize their family and personal lives over work now than they would have been before the pandemic.[1] As people embrace hybrid and remote work, renewed focus is needed to best manage work–life integration challenges. Organizations and HR teams should realize that they need solutions that redesign the way that people work. Already today, there are an inexhaustible number of options available in tech to increase well-being, such as subscriptions to content and apps for exercise, mental health, diet, stress, and personal finances. However, the question remains: is this technology really helpful?

It is clear that no matter how many well-being tools and perks an organization adds, they will not counterbalance the work that is burning employees out and the leadership that is viewed as untrustworthy. Employee experience is not something you buy or can merely add. It needs to reflect the culture of the company. Technology is needed, but the importance is *right* technology, and it needs to be of high quality.

What Is Employee Well-Being?

Employee well-being refers to the physical, mental, financial, and emotional health and overall satisfaction of employees in the workplace. It encompasses a wide range of factors, such as work–life integration (also referred to as work–life balance), job satisfaction, physical and mental health, and access to support and resources. Employers who prioritize employee well-being often implement policies and programs that support the physical, mental, financial, and emotional well-being of their employees and create a positive and supportive work environment.

A neurophysiological review of work–life integration challenges suggests that well-being is a highly personalized path based on one's goals, pursuits, roles, and circumstances.[2] Recommendations include developing plans for career growth, establishing expectations and boundaries early, delegating tasks, and prioritizing self-care. Technology can be of great help when creating these paths, especially when it comes to creating more personalized paths and optimizing employees' well-being through a custom employee experience.

However, a personalized experience comes with high costs, and organizations do not always see the benefits of investing in employees' well-being. However, in many countries, the labor market is tight, which forces organizations to be more creative in retaining their talents, including preventing sick leave by avoiding burnout and protecting employees' well-being. The well-being of employees has a big impact on an organization's goals and can be central to ensuring the continued success of a business. Distressed employees are ineffective for eight days per month due to decreased productivity; they may be at work, but employees struggling with mental health issues are less than half as effective as healthy employees.[3] Employees can be physically present but mentally absent, totally distancing themselves from their colleagues and the organization. The cost of a disengaged employee equals around 18 percent of their salary.[4] These costs could actually make it worthwhile for organizations to invest in a personalized well-being experience to prevent ineffectiveness and disengagement. Research has shown that such experiences bring great benefits to organizations that focus on employee well-being. Companies that enhance employees' well-being have 25 percent greater profitability and significantly higher customer satisfaction.[5]

Burnout

In 2019, the World Health Organization (WHO) officially recognized burnout in its international classification of diseases, not as a medical condition but as an occupational phenomenon.[6] The workplace is the number one stressor for American adults,[7] costing the U.S. economy roughly 300 billion dollars annually. The employee burnout crisis had already begun by 2017,[8] and the 2020 pandemic further eroded employee well-being.[9] Overall, in the United States, 30 percent of frontline and information workers said that the pandemic increased their feelings of burnout at work. In a research conducted prior to the pandemic, out of 1,000 full-time U.S. professionals, 91 percent said that unmanageable stress or frustration negatively impacted their performance, whereas 69 percent felt that their employer did not do enough to minimize burnout.[10] Work demands increasingly more from employees. To a large extent, these increasing demands fall under the intensification of work, which involves an increase in output for each hour worked or an increase in the qualitative or quantitative demands of work.[11] This intensification is characterized by a need to work faster and with shorter deadlines, a decrease in "free time," and the need to perform multiple tasks at the same time. The causes of this intensification are very diverse: globalization and increasing competition, constant technological change, increasing customer demands, increasing flexibility in the labor market, blurring boundaries between work life and private life, HR practices that encourage employee involvement and commitment, and increased standards for and expectations of the employees themselves. Due to such a multiplicity of causes, the intensification of work is not easy to reverse. The aforementioned studies and others all show a clear, steady increase in work pressure problems and burnout complaints. Despite all of the positive psychological perspectives on happiness at work and the extensive psychological knowledge available in the field of work and well-being, work conditions have not improved for many, and the COVID-19 pandemic only helped worsen conditions.

Well-being is becoming an increasingly important topic in the workplace, especially with more millennials and Generation Z entering the workplace. These generations are more likely to prioritize their mental and physical health over their career goals and look for workplaces that align with their values and support their overall well-being. Gallup's State of the Global Workplace Report found that millennials and Generation Z members are more likely to rank an employer's concern for well-being as the most important aspect they are looking for in an organization.[12]

The Impact of Multitasking

Technology and new media channels create an increasing daily need to multitask. When employees are working and they receive a notification from Facebook or Instagram that someone liked their post, they immediately stop what they were doing and start checking the notification. The 2022 Connectivity and Mobile Trends Insights of Deloitte shared that on average, we check our phones 47 times[13] a day, and for people who use the RescueTime app* it was even more: 58 times a day, including 30 times during the workday.[14] In addition, during the workday, employees receive notifications at the bottom of their computer screens when, for example, receiving a new e-mail; this too leads to multitasking. When working with my customers, their data showed that when online meetings involve large groups or are held for a long period of time, employees often start to multitask by starting to chat or e-mail during the meetings. Many people think that they can perform as many as three tasks at once, and only a limited number of people suspect that multitasking makes them less productive. Multitasking is oftentimes perceived as a woman's domain. A woman, particularly with children, will routinely juggle a job with running a household, and in a household, parents already multitask, for example, when making lunch, doing chores, and organizing the social lives of their children. Studies show that women are not better at multitasking than man; rather, they just do more work.[15] The expectation of doing more work often ties back to the burnout phenomenon, mentioned earlier in this chapter. In today's fast-paced society, the pressure to constantly achieve and exceed expectations has become pervasive. The increasing prevalence of burnout among individuals of all genders reflects the toll that excessive workloads and relentless expectations can take on mental and physical well-being. People who think that they are excellent at multitasking often give the example that they can carry on a conversation while driving. Indeed, most people can have a conversation while

---

* RescueTime is a fully automated time-tracking app that helps its users retake control of their time. The app has over two million users and has logged over 1.36 billion hours of screen time and blocked millions of distractions for its users. It helps its customers to be less distracted and more productive.

behind the wheel, but when they suddenly have to hit the brakes, most of them are unable to continue chatting.

Unfortunately, the reason for why we are poor at multitasking is not yet exactly known. There is a theory that our brains process information serially and not in a parallel manner. Simply put, we do not carry out actions at the same time but rather one after the other. Because our brains switch from one task to another at lightning speed, it seems as if we are focusing on both at the same time. Multitasking makes employees less efficient. When they are multitasking, all tasks are more or less active and require mental capacity. If different tasks require the same resources, inefficiency occurs. However, when it comes to two completely different tasks, such as doodling while participating in a meeting, the brain taps into different capacities, and in fact, employees might even better remember the meeting's content. In contrast, e-mailing during a meeting might have the opposite effect.

Multitasking can be a drawback of modern technology. Technology creates an endless to-do list, so people constantly switch between tasks. This multitasking puts pressure on the stress systems in our brains. The continuous stimulation of this system causes an increase in respiratory and heart rates. The tension in our muscles increases, and in the long term, that tension can be harmful to our brains. People who suffer from chronic stress are quite forgetful, and they often have trouble concentrating. When people are constantly answering messages and e-mails, listening to voicemails, and following news stories, the brains have neither the time nor the space to process so much information, store it in their memory, play with the ideas, and be creative. Of course, it is not easy to go offline. It is fun to be online, and we want to be up to date. Otherwise, we are afraid of missing out. People are also naturally accustomed to receiving quick responses. Employees who have become used to always being online will not find it easy to stop.

The stress system is especially made for acute stress and not for chronic stress. Acute stress is experienced, for example, when someone suddenly must brake hard on the highway. Chronic stress, on the other hand, comes with the continuous stream of new apps, e-mails, and push notifications. The opposite of multitasking is focusing on a single task, also known as monotasking. When attention is focused on a single task, one can enter a certain flow. This can happen when playing sports, reading, or writing; time can be forgotten and the task at hand becomes easier. A flow is much more effective than multitasking. A flow cannot be completely forced, but there are resources that can help facilitate one to being more focused on a single task, so that work becomes easier and more effective, avoiding all of the distractions that cause stress to the body. Multitasking is often perceived as the ability to handle multiple tasks simultaneously, but its nuance lies in the complexity of attention it requires. Attention can be categorized in different types, as illustrated in Figure 3.1.

- *Focused attention* refers to concentrating on a single task or stimulus, allowing for deep engagement and concentration. Focused attention allows employees to direct their cognitive resources toward a specific task, enabling them to achieve a higher level of accuracy, efficiency, and understanding. Focused attention is particularly crucial for tasks that

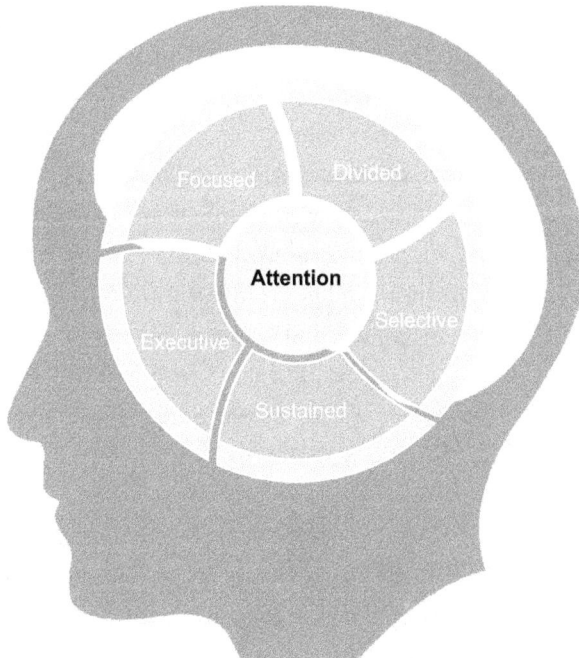

Figure 3.1 Illustration of the different types of attention

demand cognitive effort, creativity, and critical thinking. When employees direct their full attention to a single task, they achieve deeper engagement and enhanced information processing, and they produce a higher-quality outcome. It is in these focused moments that employees can truly immerse themselves in the task at hand and maximize their productivity and performance.

- *Divided attention* involves attempting to process or engage with multiple tasks or stimuli concurrently. It is important when employees attempt to process and engage with multiple activities concurrently, such as listening to a podcast while working on a spreadsheet or responding to e-mails while participating in a virtual meeting. Divided attention is often required in situations where tasks are relatively simple or automated, allowing individuals to allocate some attentional resources to each task.

- *Selective attention* refers to the ability to focus on specific stimuli while filtering out irrelevant or distracting information. It allows employees to direct their attention to important cues or tasks while disregarding others. Selective attention plays a crucial role in tasks that require prioritization and concentration, enabling employees to allocate cognitive resources effectively.

- *Sustained attention* refers to the ability to maintain focus and concentration on a task over an extended period. It involves sustaining attentional resources and resisting distractions or fatigue. Sustained attention is essential for tasks that require prolonged mental effort or vigilance, as it ensures consistent and uninterrupted engagement.

- *Executive attention* involves higher-order cognitive processes and encompasses a range of abilities, including task switching, cognitive flexibility, and inhibitory control. It enables employees to manage multiple tasks, switch between them, and regulate their attention effectively. Executive attention is crucial for complex, goal-directed activities that involve planning, decision making, and problem solving.

While multitasking may involve elements of divided attention, selective attention, sustained attention, and executive attention, all play important roles in determining how effectively employees can manage multiple tasks. Recognizing the nuances of these different types of attention can help organizations better understand the complexities of multitasking and make informed decisions about tasks prioritization, workflow management, and optimizing the employees' cognitive resources and how tools and technologies could facilitate this.

Focus Time

Focus time is important for employees, because it allows them to work on important tasks without distractions. The ability to focus on a single task for an extended period is crucial for achieving high levels of productivity and creativity. When employees can focus on their work without interruption, they are able to think more deeply and make better decisions. Additionally, having dedicated focus time can help reduce stress and burnout by allowing employees to take breaks and recharge. By providing employees with focused work time, employers can create a more positive work environment and improve employee well-being. Moreover, when employees can focus on their work, they are able to work more efficiently and complete tasks more quickly, which help improve productivity and can lead to an increase in job satisfaction and motivation. Technologies can help prevent multitasking and improve the focus of employees.

- Focus apps and browser extensions block distracting websites and apps during designated periods of time. Some organizations even have one or two meeting-free days, allowing employees to focus on their work.
- Some tools and apps use timed intervals of work and rest to improve focus and productivity. These apps can also act as a "Do not disturb" sign by allowing employees to block off focus time in their calendars, which prevents their receiving notifications and thus eliminates distractions.
- Mindfulness and meditation apps, such as Headspace, teach users to be more present and mindful, reducing distractions and increasing focus.

- Virtual and augmented reality technologies can be used to create immersive experiences that reduce distractions and improve focus.
- Time management apps help users prioritize tasks and manage their time more efficiently.
- AI-based productivity tools can help employees improve the quality of their work and reduce their time spent on editing and proofreading.
- The settings for how messages are delivered in your organizations can be optimized. Communication apps for e-mails and instant messages have a feature to allow for asynchronous work, meaning that a sent message will be delivered during the recipient's working hours and not the sender's.

Another reason why it can be hard to focus is *precrastination*, which is choosing to act on something sooner rather than later. At work, precrastination is seen when employees answer an e-mail as soon as it arrives, often at the cost of other tasks. One of the big challenges with precrastination is that it can disrupt an otherwise well-planned day and even lead to stress.[16]

The Importance of Leadership Behavior in Preventing Multitasking

Leadership behavior plays a critical role in preventing multitasking and promoting focus within an organization. Leaders set the tone for their entire organization, and their behavior can have a significant impact in the way that their employees work. Leadership behavior plays a key role in creating a culture of focus within an organization. By modeling good behavior, encouraging focus time, and communicating the importance of focus, leaders can prevent multitasking and improve productivity. My former team at Microsoft analyzed how people analytics can give insights into leadership behaviors, and we found that leaders' work habits are copied by their team members. When managers work on the weekend or late at night, they send the signal to their teams that this behavior is also expected of them. The other interesting thing that we found is when leaders send e-mails during meetings, their direct reports are 2.2 times more likely to copy that behavior.[17] When leaders and managers work late nights or weekends, they could include a message in their signature stating that they work asynchronously and that employees need not reply if they receive the message out of their normal working hours. People analytics can help to assess during what meetings employees multitask and how often and if they copy their leaders' behaviors, as had happened in the aforementioned example. These insights could also contribute to making meetings more effective and ensuring that the right audience is present. This could lead to the employees' not being overworked by multitasking all day and thus an increase in their well-being.

Collaboration Overload

Collaboration overload, also known as collaboration fatigue, is a growing issue in today's workplace and can have a negative impact on employees' well-being. It refers to the negative impact of too much collaboration, including excessive meetings, e-mails, and instant messages, on an individual's well-being. It can cause stress, burnout, decreased job satisfaction, and decreased productivity. Constant collaboration can lead to a feeling of being "always on" and never having a chance to disconnect, which can be overwhelming and exhausting. Additionally, too many collaboration demands can lead to an excessive workload, leaving employees feeling overwhelmed and unable to balance their professional and personal responsibilities. Ironically, collaboration overload can lead to decreased productivity. Constant interruptions of meetings can disrupt an individual's workflow, making it difficult to complete tasks efficiently. This can lead to a feeling of being overwhelmed and a sense of not getting things done, leading to decreased motivation and job satisfaction. Collaboration overload can also lead to decreased creativity. When individuals are constantly collaborating, they may feel pressure to conform to group dynamics and ideas, leading to a lack of creative thinking and innovation. This can lead to a feeling of stagnation and a lack of personal growth and development.

A *Harvard Business Review* study found that it was not only the always-on culture; encroaching technology, demanding bosses, or clients; or inefficient coworkers that played a significant role in the problem, but also the individual's own mindset and work habits. "Knowing why you accept collaborative work—above and beyond what your manager and company demand—is how you begin to combat overload."[18] One of my executives at LinkedIn always said: "it is the things you say no to that allow you to do things you say yes to *right*." Unfortunately, we are not always aware of our own or our team's behavior. Behavioral signals can give insights into individuals', teams', and organizations' behaviors. At Microsoft, these insights helped our customers understand what behaviors put pressure on different teams and what behaviors could be changed in order to reduce collaboration overload.

Overall, collaboration overload can lead to decreased job satisfaction. When individuals are overwhelmed and stressed, they are less likely to enjoy their work and thus feel fulfilled by their job. This can lead to increased turnover rates and decreased motivation and engagement. Collaboration overload can have a significant impact on an individual's well-being. To mitigate these negative effects, it is important for organizations to establish clear communication protocols and guidelines, prioritize and manage workloads effectively, and provide employees with appropriate support and resources. Employers can take steps to reduce collaboration overload, such as limiting meetings and e-mails, promoting work–life balance, and providing resources for stress management and mental health support. By prioritizing the well-being of their employees, employers can create a positive and productive workplace culture.

Case: The Influence of Meetings on Vitality at ING

The health and vitality of employees are oftentimes affected by bad work habits. I had the privilege of speaking with Alexander Stolze, head of vitality at ING,[†] about the influence of bad work and meeting habits on the vitality of employees. Alexander and his team are leveraging various types of data and technologies to improve

(Continues)

[†] ING is a global bank with a strong European base. It employs more than 58,000 individuals and serves around 38 million customers, corporate clients, and financial institutions in over 40 countries. Its purpose is to empower people to stay a step ahead in life and in business. More at www.ing.com.

(*Continued*)

the vitality of ING employees. Alexander states that "at ING we care about our people—vitality and resilience are key to business performance." At ING, Alexander and his team have developed a framework to enable employees to embed healthier working habits into their daily work lives. The framework was created by involving the voice of employees; surveys were conducted and focus groups were held. After months of research, a variety of topics surfaced on how vitality could be embedded into the way that employees work together at ING.

The framework that they created focuses on four aspects:

1. *Schedule respectfully*: This encourages a healthy collaboration culture where employees are asked to minimize time spent in meetings and to work more asynchronously. It allows ING employees to refocus their attention on the benefits of effective meetings to reduce anxieties about poorly prepared meetings and overcome common tendencies, such as feeling obligated to attend a meeting or to prevent forgetting to invite a stakeholder by simply just inviting everyone to a meeting.
2. *Prioritize realistically*: Within this aspect, employees are given autonomy to prioritize and set boundaries and to stick to these priorities by carving out time in their calendars.
3. *Recharge regularly*: This aspect focuses on encouraging employees to take microbreaks by scheduling meetings of 25 minutes instead of 30 and 50 minutes instead of 60. It also encourages employees to disconnect after a working day and to take lunch breaks and vacation time.
4. *Engage in social time*: This aspect focuses on the recognition and value of relationships. Employees at ING are encouraged to spend social time together.

Based on these aspects, ING is leveraging technology and influencing strategies to change the behaviors of its employees.

A few of the technologies that ING has created are simple to use but can make a big difference. A meeting template that ING created is one example. When employees are scheduling a meeting, they see the option of adding a standard meeting template to the invitation. The goal is to help the meeting organizers prepare. It not only reminds all employees that meetings should be well prepared, but also shows how a meeting is properly prepared for.

ING also provides employees insights into their meeting habits and behaviors, which help employees to actively reflect on their meeting habits and behaviors. The employees receive their insights in Microsoft Teams, and when reflecting on their habits, they receive recommended learning materials on meeting habits, all in their own flow of work.

A meeting poll in Microsoft Teams created by ING is another idea that I loved. Currently, attendees of a Microsoft Teams meeting are already asked to review the quality of the meeting, but these questions are only related to the technology of the meeting: was the quality of the sound sufficient and so on? What ING intends to do is improve the quality and effectiveness of the meetings by promoting accountability and encouraging a culture of discussing and evaluating the usefulness of meetings by having a poll at the end of every meeting to rate the real quality of the meeting. Employees can rate different aspects that are important for effective meetings. For example, they can rate the preparation of the meeting, the availability of documents, the clarity of roles of the attendees, or the participant group size.

Alexander and his team have created a plan based on the aforementioned research and are developing more solutions to help the employees of ING to be healthier and happier at work, which fits the mission of his team: "embedding vitality in how we work together."

The Four-Day Workweek

Creating a balance between paid work and family life through alternative work schedules is not a new idea, nor are the application of alternatives to 8-hour workdays and 40-hour workweeks necessarily limited to white-collar jobs. Just after the start of the Great Depression, the

Kellogg's cereal plant in Michigan, United States, replaced its three eight-hour shifts per day with four six-hour shifts. With the change, Kellogg's hoped to simultaneously achieve several goals: (1) to reduce unemployment in the community, (2) to increase worker efficiency, and (3) to provide employees greater opportunities for recreation and enjoyment outside of business hours, which would generally result in better living and working conditions.[19] Though this type of alternative workday did not become popular after the Great Depression, and with the rise of technology, it has gained popularity in recent years. A four-day workweek involves reducing the traditional five-day workweek to four days, allowing employees to have an extra day off each week. While the concept may seem enticing to employees, it is important to consider both the advantages and disadvantages of this arrangement in terms of employee well-being.

There are many benefits, not only of a four-day workweek but also of having reduced hours during the workday. Transitioning from a time-focused model to a task-focused model can bring more flexibility for employees to do unpaid work, such as caring for parents or children and completing household chores, or to have more leisure time. Experimenting with different versions of reduced hours, such as a four-day workweek or spreading 32 hours across seven days, can bring benefits for both the employer and the employee.

- *Reduced stress and burnout*: Employees who work fewer days or hours a week have more time to rest and recover from work-related stress. With an extra day off each week, they can focus on personal activities and hobbies, which can help improve mental health and reduce the risk of burnout. The improved work–life balance could make individuals plan their lives less around work and more around life itself; life could be a workcation. A four-day workweek can help employees better manage their work and personal responsibilities. This can result in a more balanced lifestyle, which can lead to better physical and mental health.
- *Increased productivity*: Some studies have suggested that reducing the workweek can lead to increased productivity.

At Microsoft, during the "Work Life Choice Challenge 2019 Summer," we experimented in Japan with a four-day workweek. Overall, the change led to a 40 percent increase in productivity, and it reduced electricity use in offices and the number of pages printed by employees.[20] When employees have more time to rest and recharge, they may be more focused and productive during their actual working hours.

• *Attracting and retaining talent*: Offering a four-day workweek can be an attractive perk for employees, particularly younger workers who value work–life balance. This can help companies attract and retain top talent.

There are also downsides or challenges associated with a four-day work week. Not all professions allow for scheduling a four-day work week. For example, nurses, truck drivers, and cabin crews work long shifts, and their work cannot be fit into a more traditional way of scheduling. Different categories of workers have different needs. Individuals who work for minimum wage need to have enough hours to make a living wage. A four-day workweek should not further increase the inequity between information workers and frontline workers. Another complexity also arises: if employers allow employees their one day off on different days of the week, organizations need to ensure there is enough coverage to deliver, for example, in a customer service department. Allowing the spread of one-day-off can lead to frustration of colleagues, especially initially as collaborative tasks may take longer to complete. Employees, regardless of their professions, do desire more flexibility and more choice, but it does need to fit within the profession of the employee and cannot be fully driven by personal choice. As mentioned in Chapter 2, a different type of schedule needs to suit the individual preferences and fit within the team values and organizational boundaries.

The hard part is to determine how to measure success and productivity. It is easier for managers to measure time than performance. The latter requires a different type of skills for managers. As mentioned in Chapter 1, automation and leveraging chatbots could be utilized to maintain 24/7 services for customers, while freeing up time for employees. HR systems also need to be agile to accommodate for the flexibility needs of employees. Experimenting with what works for different workers and organizations is the way forward.

Employers should carefully evaluate whether or not a 4-day or 32-hour workweek is feasible for their organization and work with their employees to ensure that scheduling arrangements meet the needs of both parties. However, with the right technology, we can increase output and productivity while simultaneously reducing working hours. Organizations have acquired the technology to make us work better and feel better; however, we use such technology infrequently or poorly. With the help of technology, we can provide different ways of working and create prosperity, not by working more hours but rather by increasing productivity through our interactions with innovation and technology.

External Factors That Are a Risk for Employee Well-Being

Not all stressors in a person's life are related to work. Life-changing events, such as the death of a loved one, divorce, job loss, illness, or relocation, can have a significant impact on an individual's well-being. These events can also cause stress, anxiety, and depression and can lead to physical health problems. Not all can be solved by technology; however, employers can improve external factors in their employees' lives to improve their well-being in some ways.

Financial Health

Organizations are taking more responsibility and actions regarding the financial health of their employees. Financial concerns are a major source of stress among employees. According to the PwC Financial Wellness survey, 59 percent of employees say finances cause the bulk of their stress and 35 percent of employees are distracted by their finances while at work.[21] Financial stress can have a negative effect on an employee's physical and mental health, job performance, sleep, and overall well-being. Employers can help alleviate this stress by providing resources and support to help employees manage their finances. There are different apps available to address different financial concerns and needs, from apps that help employees set aside funds from their salary to save toward their children's college tuition to apps that help employees manage their own debt. It is important to note that the effects of financial well-being at work can vary for each individual depending upon their specific circumstances. Therefore, it is important to pay attention to the specific needs of employees, leverage technology, and tailor programs accordingly.

Sleep

In modern society where being always available and constantly hyper-connected is expected, many people lose sleep, which causes challenges in life and at work. Sleep is an essential aspect of our well-being, and poor sleep can significantly impact our productivity, mood, and health. Leaders who claim to thrive and be very productive with only four hours of sleep are an exception, and neuroscience research actually contradicts their claims. Leadership behavior relies on executive functions, such as problem solving, reasoning, organizing, planning, and executing plans, and these functions all depend upon a part of our brain that needs sleep to function well.[22] A study from McKinsey also highlighted a strong correlation between leadership performance and organizational health.[23] Leadership performance and organizational health are strong predictors of the bottom line because they both have a direct impact on the overall success of an organization. When leadership performance and organizational health are strong, organizations are more likely to achieve their financial objectives, increase revenue, and improve profitability. Employers can play a crucial role in helping their employees sleep better by facilitating the use of technologies and apps, such as sleep tracking apps, blue light filters, relaxation, or mindfulness apps, that promote healthy sleep habits. Employers can also consider providing sleep pods or nap rooms in which employees can take a short nap during the workday. These pods can be equipped with ambient noise, comfortable lighting, and temperature controls to promote a better nap. It is important when enabling employees to create healthier habits to provide the right tools while respecting the employees' privacy.

Lack of Movement

Prolonged periods of sitting or inactivity have been linked to a range of health problems, including obesity, cardiovascular disease, and type 2 diabetes. When employees sit for long periods of time without movement, it can increase their risk of developing health problems and can lead to decreased productivity and higher health care costs for the organization. In addition, a lack of physical movement can lead to decreased energy and focus, which can negatively impact job performance.

To address the lack of movement and the imbalance of calories consumed, organizations can encourage employees to take short breaks to move and stretch throughout the day, provide ergonomic equipment, and offer wellness programs that encourage physical activity and healthy habits. The implementation of healthy food programs can be a great way to encourage employees to eat more healthily at work. There are tools that can help analyze which healthy foods are popular among employees to predict what other healthy foods employees might like. Leveraging these tools and predictions can help to increase healthy habits.

There are several benefits to encouraging employees to be more physically active and to avoid sitting for extended periods of time. Regular physical activity can reduce the risk of some chronic diseases, including heart disease and diabetes. Physical activity can increase energy levels and boost cognitive function, which can lead to increased productivity. Exercise is also a natural stress reliever and can help to reduce feelings of anxiety and depression. During my first few jobs, I installed a program on my computer that every so often locked my screen and forced me to do certain exercises, such as arm movements or squats, to prevent me from developing back problems. Technologies luckily have evolved to encourage employees to move more often, without disrupting their flow abruptly, and some are described next.

- *Stand-up desks*: These desks can be adjusted so that employees can work while standing, which can help to reduce the amount of time that they spend sitting.
- *Walking meetings*: Instead of holding meetings while sitting, employees can hold meetings while walking. In 2022, at a

Vitality Congress, Marieke van Beurden, who manages the Workplace Vitality Hub,[‡] proposed an interesting solution. On campus, her company created several routes, each with a specific duration time. Instead of booking a meeting room for a 30-minute, one-on-one meeting, employees could schedule a route that takes 30 minutes to complete. One step further would be for the booking system to inform employees whether they had not yet been on a walk that day and accordingly suggest booking a walking meeting. Another further development could be to integrate the weather forecast so that employees could schedule their walks accordingly.

- *Activity trackers*: Wearable devices like fitness trackers can help employees monitor their physical activity levels and set goals to increase them. Employers can provide the wearables or subscriptions, but should not have the intent to use these as monitoring tools.

In this way, technology can help in encouraging employees to be more physically active and make healthier lifestyle choices, and it can enable organizations to make employee wellness programs more personalized.

Case: How Exoskeletons Improve the Well-Being of Employees

An exoskeleton is a wearable device designed to enhance human performance and assist with physical tasks. The use of an exoskeleton can improve an employee's well-being by reducing physical strain. The skeleton provides additional support and reduces the weight of heavy loads, which can help in reducing physical strain and fatigue

(Continues)

[‡] Located on the High Tech Campus Eindhoven, The Netherlands, the Workplace Vitality Hub offers space for collaborative research and development into vitality at work solutions, enabled by smart technologies. Founding partners are Fontys, imec, TNO, Eindhoven University of Technology, High Tech Campus Eindhoven, and TWICE.

(Continued)

and the risk of musculoskeletal injuries. It can also improve body posture by providing support to the back and joints, reducing the risk of chronic pain and discomfort. By increasing strength and endurance, exoskeletons can enhance an employee's performance, leading to increased job satisfaction and reduced feelings of stress and burnout.

A pilot program at a beverage warehouse organized and monitored by Timing[§] showed that when using an exoskeleton, employees experienced less physical strain at work, and as a result they experienced higher job satisfaction. Before the pilot, 100 percent of the employees raised some type of physical complaint related to work. The majority of complaints were about pain in their shoulders, arms, elbows, back, chest, or knees. Overall, 75 percent of the respondents indicated that they would change jobs if they were to receive an offer for a job that is less physically demanding. After the use of an exoskeleton, respondents reported to have experienced the following benefits: their backs were no longer burdened, they had straight back support, and they could maintain a better posture during work.

The pilot also showed that there is a risk to not using exoskeletons correctly. If an exoskeleton is not used correctly, it could pose other physical challenges or cause employees to want to stop using it all together, because they do not experience the benefits. The pilot also showed that adapting to new ways of working is hard and was received differently by different individuals. Receiving clear training is needed for employees to experience the full benefits of an exoskeleton. Overall, the study reported that working with an exoskeleton contributed to a higher work motivation and a better physical well-being among employees.

[§] Timing is an employment agency with 900 fixed information workers and 25,000 frontline employees. The company believes in the power of people who perform and are committed to the appreciation of frontline work. Every day, Timing employs more than 25,000 flex and payroll workers, from production workers to cleaners, ensuring that the Dutch economy continues to run. More at www.timing.nl.

Impact of Recognition on Well-Being

Employee recognition is an essential aspect of creating a positive and productive work environment. The positive effects of recognition can benefit both employees and organizations as a whole. When employees feel recognized and appreciated for their contributions, they are more likely to experience positive emotions, such as satisfaction, pride, and motivation. This in turn leads to higher levels of well-being, which include physical health, emotional health, and social well-being. According to a 2022 study, recognition is linked to improved well-being in four major areas:

1. Increased overall life evaluations
2. Improved daily emotions
3. Reduced levels of burnout
4. Better social well-being[24]

Another positive effect of recognition is increased job satisfaction. Employees who feel recognized are more likely to feel satisfied with their jobs, which leads to higher levels of engagement and commitment. Employees are also more likely to have positive attitudes toward their work, colleagues, and organizations. Value-based recognition helps employees to find greater meaning in their work and also to establish more trust in their leadership (if it happens on a regular basis and not only with an annual review or annual bonus).[25]

There are various technologies that organizations can use to create a culture of employee recognition. Employee recognition software allows managers and colleagues to recognize employees for their achievements, milestones, and contributions. There are also special recognition platforms that provide a social media-like interface for employees to recognize and celebrate each other's achievements. In daily software programs used for everyday work, there are also options to recognize individual or team achievements and to show appreciation for employees. These apps and technologies can help organizations to create a culture of employee recognition and appreciation. By using these tools, managers and colleagues can recognize employees for their contributions, celebrate their achievements, and foster a positive workplace culture. Organizations that prioritize employee recognition and create a culture of appreciation are more likely to have a happy, engaged, and productive workforce.

Psychological Safety

Psychological safety in the workplace refers to a culture where all employees feel safe to express themselves without fear of negative consequences, such as ridicule, rejection, or retaliation. It is a shared belief that it is safe to take interpersonal risks, such as speaking up with ideas, questions, concerns, or mistakes, without being punished or humiliated.

Psychological safety promotes open communication, trust, collaboration, and learning. It encourages employees to be authentic, creative, and innovative. When psychological safety is present, team members feel valued and respected, leading to higher job satisfaction, engagement, and productivity.

Psychological safety is especially important in industries where there are high-stakes decisions, complex tasks, or potential risks to health and safety. For example, in health care, psychological safety can help reduce medical errors and improve patient outcomes. In tech, psychological safety can foster a culture of experimentation and learning from failures.

While technology and apps cannot completely replace the human element of creating a culture of psychological safety in the workplace, there are a few tools that can help promote safety in the workplace, such as anonymous feedback tools. These collaboration tools, which make it easier for people to share ideas and ask questions or to give feedback, can also help in breaking down hierarchical barriers that may prevent employees from speaking up.

Organizational network analysis (ONA) is a method that can be used to analyze the social networks and communication patterns within an organization. ONA can help identify the informal networks that exist within the formal structure of an organization and provide insights into how information flows, collaboration occurs, and decisions are made. By analyzing the communication patterns within these networks, ONA can also help uncover the level of psychological safety within an organization.

- ONA can help identify who is communicating with whom, how frequently, and about what. By analyzing these communication patterns, organizations can identify which teams or individuals are more connected and which are more isolated.
- ONA can help measure the level of trust within an organization by analyzing the strength and frequency of the relationships between individuals. Doing so can give organizations a sense of whether or not certain individuals or groups feel safe to express their opinions or share their ideas. Stronger relationships between individuals may indicate higher levels of trust and psychological safety.
- ONA can help identify bottlenecks in communication and collaboration. If certain individuals or teams are central to the communication flow, this may indicate that other individuals or teams are not communicating effectively, and thus this is where psychological safety might be lacking.
- ONA can help identify informal networks within an organization, such as groups of employees who share common interests or values. These informal networks can provide insight into how psychological safety is perceived within the organization and can help identify employees who may be key influencers in promoting a culture of psychological safety.

By using ONA to uncover the level of psychological safety within an organization, targeted interventions to promote a culture of open communication, trust, and collaboration can be developed. Ultimately, the success of these tools in promoting psychological safety depends on how they are implemented and integrated into the workplace culture. It is important to use them in ways that encourage open communication, respect, and empathy. I will share more about ONA in Chapter 5.

Implementing Well-Being Technology and Programs

Gartner's 2021 Employee Value Proposition survey shows that 87 percent of employees have access to mental and emotional well-being programs, yet only 21 percent of the employees actually participate.[26] According to the WHO, involving a lifestyle program's target group in its design and implementation is one of the critical success factors.[27] By involving employees in design and implementation, their experiences can be properly considered. With interventions, it is wise to involve employees at an early stage in the design and implementation, for example, by collecting ideas and requests in focus groups. Some organizations benefit by implementing well-being technology and programs within their sector. With a sectorwide approach, it is important that technologies and programs can be tailored to the needs of individual companies and the various needs of employee groups within companies. Allowing individual employees to make choices from a wide range of options can also increase support for interventions.

It is sometimes difficult to create a healthy group culture within a company. Nevertheless, some companies seem to succeed in establishing a healthy group culture. Ways that companies often achieve this include the following.

- Involving employees in the design and implementation of the program. There are many tools and apps available that could help in gaining input from a broad set of employees for brainstorming.
- Appointing a few pioneers within the company. People analytics could help in identifying who these pioneers should be.
- Demonstrating the experiments or programs that have worked.
- Promoting frequent communication, so that it is clear to employees that the organization attaches great importance to the health of its employees.
- Gamification can be a powerful tool in fostering a healthy group culture at work. By incorporating game elements

into the workplace, organizations can motivate employees, encourage collaboration, and promote a positive work environment.

Throughout all stages of the process when creating a health policy or well-being program, it is crucial that line management is involved, as illustrated in Figure 3.2. Involving line management throughout the process enables them to also support and encourage employees to improve their lifestyles. Including a scorecard or objectives could help in incorporating all managers throughout all management layers of the organization.

On the other hand, there are also many reasons why programs can fail. Employees' uncertainty about their privacy (what will my employer do with my health data?) can be a barrier to participate in health programs. If there is too little support and too few incentives for management, an employee participating in a health program may feel insufficiently supported by their manager. This can make the employee feel alone and less inclined to share positive experiences or even stop participating altogether—both of which are missed opportunities.

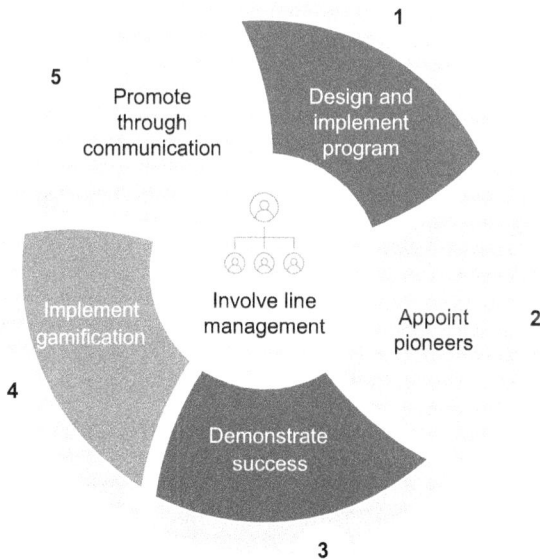

Figure 3.2 Steps in creating a healthy group culture

Companies can benefit from introducing in-work health interventions. An in-work health intervention refers to a proactive approach taken by organizations to promote and improve the health and well-being of their employees while they are at work. These interventions are designed to address various aspects of health, including physical, mental, and emotional well-being. The specific nature of an in-work health intervention may vary depending on the organization, its resources, and the specific needs of its employees. The success of an intervention depends on several factors, such as to what degree the intervention suits the target group and whether or not it has been properly implemented. Developing an intervention not as a one-size-fits-all, but tailored to suit the target groups, contributes to the more personalized employee experience. Since the implementation of health interventions is a complex task involving multiple layers of an organization, the HR department plays a crucial role. Overall, it should have a coordinating role in the implementation of vitality programs and interventions. Good communication and coordination internally and externally with the intervention providers are the biggest success factors during implementation. In addition, the HR department can contribute specific knowledge to cross-sectoral approaches, and interventions and programs can then be implemented at a companywide or even industrywide level. An industrywide approach is beneficial for smaller businesses, as they have relatively smaller budgets to spend on these types of programs, and well-being is not always their top priority. Another argument for industry focus could be that small and medium businesses often have a small (or no) HR department, and no policies are made in the field of well-being.

The Impact of Technology on the Well-Being of Frontline Workers

While most of the examples mentioned in this chapter have covered information workers, there are also many developments that can impact the well-being of frontline workers in several ways. With technology such as wearable devices and personal protective equipment, employees can stay safe in hazardous environments. Technology can also help frontline workers perform their jobs more efficiently and reduce the physical and mental stress associated with manual tasks. Smartphones and instant messaging technologies can help frontline workers stay in touch with colleagues and managers, which can reduce feelings of isolation.

Technology can also help frontline workers manage and organize their data more effectively, reducing the risk of errors and the stress associated with data management. Virtual and augmented reality technologies can provide workers with new training opportunities, reducing the risk of injury and increasing their overall well-being. However, for frontline workers, technology could also have a negative impact on their well-being, such as by decreasing face-to-face interaction and increasing screen time, and the fear of job changes due to AI, which could lead to physical and mental health challenges. Therefore, it is important, when implementing new technologies, to keep assessing the risks and the benefits. Especially with emerging technologies for frontline workers, leaders, even if they have positive intentions, can really misunderstand the impact that the acquired technologies can have on their employees. Unless leaders understand what is happening on the frontline, it is sometimes hard to understand the real needs of frontline workers. Companies are spending large parts of their budgets on technology, but these technologies are not always bringing the intended value to their employees. I spoke about this disconnect with Alex Bertram, who has spent his career in placing emerging technologies in the hands of frontline workers in the energy and resources industry, with a focus on frontline safety. He shared a few examples on how technology has impacted the well-being of frontline workers in this industry.

Case: Emerging Technology for Frontline Workers in the Mining and Resource Industry

One of the core platforms that Alex Bertram and his team developed was called Dash Tools. Dash was a system of sensors, like an IT system, that was retrofitted to heavy mining equipment. Before the system was established, frontline workers had been exposed to many elements that had impacted their safety. The employees had

(*Continues*)

(*Continued*)

worked in an environment with a temperature of 40°C to 45°C and had operated machines, trucks, diggers, and excavators as big as two-to-three story houses. The employees had worked 12-hour shifts in a heavy industrial environment, onsite for multiple days in a row. Dash was ultimately developed to reduce fatality rates. The new system enabled mechanics to perform diagnostic work on machines without having to be exposed to all the elements.

Besides safety issues, the employees had also struggled with large overhead costs. Due to the dangerous environment, there had been many processes and protocols in place to ensure safety, which had created overhead that employees needed to deal with on a daily basis to operate the heavy machinery. Employees needed to conduct risk assessments, which dragged supervisors and superintendents out of their work to sign off on paperwork. This process can add a lot of extra work and potential stress to someone's day. Dash reduced this overhead and also employees' exposure to the external elements, creating far less extra work and stress.

When I interviewed Alex, we spoke about the effects of the COVID-19 pandemic on frontline work in the resource and mining industry. In Australia, and elsewhere in the world, the pandemic did not allow people to travel to the worksite. Leveraging mixed reality and HoloLens headsets in support of product development at the beginning of the pandemic became common. People who could not be sent to the worksite ended up using HoloLens headsets to visit the site remotely, working with the teams that were still onsite and on the frontline. Because in this industry people need to be frontline and their work cannot be done remotely, the pandemic accelerated the application of methods for carrying out tasks differently. The risk of not acting and not adapting was greater than the risk of trying new methods. After Alex successfully implemented Dash for his team, his company scaled the application to other parts of the organization.

It is interesting that when the pandemic restrictions were lifted, the need for mixed reality stayed, while some tasks resorted back to their prepandemic state. Remote work methods were not a permanent solution, and being onsite in this industry cannot be fully replaced with the use of technology. Alex also mentioned that, in the industry, the terms of certain contracts and agreements are not compatible with fully remote work. For example, warrantees on equipment sometimes state that the warrantee is only valid if a technician is physically present. However, being able to do the work partly remote is an improvement to employees' well-being. Another interesting fact is that the Dash project was business driven, and it involved senior management, a few IT people, and HR. When scaling Dash to the whole organization, HR played a crucial role in streamlining processes and ensuring compliance with company policy.

Case: Autonomous Trucks

Alex and I also discussed the topic of autonomous trucks. Autonomous trucks have the potential to also positively impact employee well-being in several ways. They can help to reduce the risk of accidents and injuries that are often associated with mining operations. Mining sites are typically large and complex, with heavy machinery and vehicles moving around constantly, which can be hazardous for human operators. By removing the need for human drivers, autonomous trucks can help to reduce the risk of accidents and create a safer working environment for employees. Autonomous trucks can help to reduce the physical strain and fatigue associated with operating heavy machinery. Mining trucks are typically very large and require a lot of physical effort to operate, which can lead to strain on the body and an increased risk of injury. Autonomous trucks can alleviate this by allowing operators to control the trucks from a remote location, reducing the physical demands of the job and creating a safer and more comfortable environment. Autonomous trucks can also help increase productivity by reducing downtime and allowing for a more efficient use of resources. With autonomous trucks, operators can

(*Continues*)

(*Continued*)

monitor multiple vehicles at once and ensure that they are running at optimal efficiency, reducing the need for manual monitoring and maintenance.

People fear that moving to more autonomous technologies means that there are fewer people needed for jobs, resulting in people being fired. Currently, the field of autonomous trucks is still small, but many people fear that autonomous trucks will take their jobs. While autonomous trucks are a huge investment, they can improve employee well-being without necessarily reducing the number of jobs. The total number of jobs when an organization implements working with autonomous trucks tends to be higher than when organizations are solely working with traditional, nonautonomous trucks. With an autonomous system, there is no longer a need to have the truck drivers driving the trucks; this reduces the need for that type of employees. However, there are many other skills required to keep autonomous trucks functioning. There are a variety of skills needed to keep these trucks running and that sometimes leads to employing more people than the organization had before they invested in autonomous trucks. The skill set needed for working with autonomous trucks is different and more complex, and this brings an opportunity for employees to be upskilled. Some of the employees would stay involved in both the autonomous system and in the other nonautonomous supporting roles.

To run an autonomous truck or a system of trucks at or to a mine site, a digital twin** of the hall roads needs to be built and maintained. For that, people called builders who build a digital replica of the physical environment and ensure that the replica stays current are needed. In Alex's experience, he has seen drivers move into these differently skilled roles. Overall, there are many jobs that implementing autonomous systems creates. The use of autonomous trucks on mining sites can contribute to employee well-being by

---

** Simply put, a digital twin is the digital counterpart of a physical object; more details will be covered in Chapter 6.

reducing the risk of accidents and injuries, reducing the physical strain and fatigue, and increasing productivity. By creating a safer and more comfortable working environment, autonomous trucks can help to improve job satisfaction and overall well-being of employees in the mining industry.

Conclusion

Employees are increasingly prioritizing well-being. HR leaders need to respond accordingly by ensuring that existing well-being programs have higher participation rates and by fundamentally redesigning work and people processes to create a human-centric culture with empathy at its core.

With more technology entering the workplace, employees are facing difficulties in dividing their attention and are constantly being disrupted and distracted. With the added workloads, there is simply not enough time in a day, which makes employees see no other solution than to multitask. However, multitasking can have detrimental effects on well-being. Fragmenting attention and increasing the cognitive load can lead to decreased productivity, heightened stress levels, and reduced enjoyment of activities. Prioritizing monotasking and practicing mindfulness techniques can help promote well-being by fostering focus, reducing stress, and enhancing the overall satisfaction in the lives of employees.

Focus time is important for employees, because it allows them to work more productively and efficiently, reduces stress and burnout, and helps to improve their overall well-being. Encouraging employees to take regular breaks and to have dedicated focus time can lead to higher levels of productivity, creativity, and job satisfaction.

There is also a limit to be considered for how much data can be collected and for what purpose. The question remains: does the responsibility of health and well-being lie with the employee or the employer, or is there enough mutual trust for a joint effort? Leveraging more technology can increase productivity and free up employee's time. As organizations and as society, we need to decide whether this time will be used for *more work or more leisure.*

CHAPTER 4

Fairness at Work

Fairness at work refers to the idea that employees are treated equitably and justly by their employers. It involves ensuring that employees have equal opportunities for hiring, promotions, and pay, regardless of their race, gender, sexual orientation, or any other personal characteristic. With more technologies being used, it is important for organizations to use these tools and technologies responsibly and ethically and ensure that employees are treated just and equitably.

There are several ways that employers can promote fairness at work, including by implementing transparent policies and procedures for hiring, promotions, and compensation. Employers can create a workplace culture that values diversity and inclusion (D&I), by, for example, celebrating and respecting differences among employees, providing accommodations for employees with different abilities or special needs, and creating an environment where all employees feel safe to share their ideas and opinions. Promoting fairness at work is important for ensuring that both employees and employers contribute to the success of the organization.

Technology can be a powerful tool for promoting fairness at work. Some ways that employers can leverage technology to create a more equitable workplace are:

- *Blind hiring*: Some employers use software that removes certain information from submitted job applications, such as name, gender, and age, in order to eliminate bias and promote fairness in the hiring process.
- *Accessibility tools*: Technology can be used to provide accessibility tools, such as screen readers or voice recognition software, for employees with different abilities or special needs.

- *Data analysis*: Technology can be used to analyze workforce data and identify potential areas of bias or discrimination. For example, analytics tools can be used to analyze pay and promotion data to identify any discrepancies.

Implementing fairness at work can be very complex. The labor market is dynamic and constantly changing, and it is challenging for many organizations to keep up with the demand to be more fair and to respond adequately. For example, the demand for inclusive employment and the promotion of diversity in the workplace has increased considerably in many organizations. Including more diversity-related goals in their strategy and showing the efforts taken to reach the goals can be hard to implement for organizations. Data analysis and technology can help organizations to become more fair and to show progress toward the organizations' goals. AI capabilities can help leaders understand individuals' behaviors and how they change over time, helping the leader reinforce and optimize behaviors that promote fairness and inclusion.

The ways that technologies and data models are being created and trained upon need to be inclusive. Otherwise, organizations risk achieving the opposite result, whereby the situation is less fair than when human (biased) decisions are made. A known example of such a negative result occurred when Amazon built an AI tool to help with recruiting. Unfortunately, the tool showed bias against women. The model was trained by learning from men's resumes, and by doing so, the model learned that men's resumes were favorable to women's, which resulted in the value of women's resumes becoming downgraded and a bias toward hiring men.[1]

While HR teams often lead the diversity, equity, and inclusion (DEI) strategies for the workforce, IT leaders can play a critical role in designing, developing, and executing tech-enabled solutions to address the complex challenges and demands in the changing world of work. When both departments work together, they can identify areas that lack diversity and equity, and technology or data leaders can rethink the ways that data is collected, analyzed, managed, and reported. Data and technology leaders have the technical expertise to integrate solutions throughout the entire employee life cycle. Different apps and technologies can be seamlessly integrated into work and collaboration software, making it part of employees' daily routine. This way, the tools and apps can help in nudging employees toward more equitable behaviors throughout their daily work. For example, with performance reviews, a simple usage of such a tool could be that when a manager is preparing a review, they receive a nudge to participate in unconscious bias training, which they can access in their flow of work. A more complex example could be that performance reviews are recorded and analyzed with software to determine whether the manager used inclusive language and intonation during the review.

In this chapter, I share, throughout the employee life cycle, how technologies can help organizations to be more inclusive and fair. I also share the potential dangers of using technology for inclusion and the importance of ethical decision making when implementing these tools and technologies. Figure 4.1 illustrates technologies that support fairness at work throughout the employee life cycle.

Brand and Recruit

An inclusive employer brand is one that promotes DEI in the workplace. It is a representation of the organization's values and commitment to creating an environment where people of all backgrounds, identities, and experiences feel welcomed and supported. To create an inclusive organization, companies need to ensure that their recruitment, retention, and promotion practices are unbiased and provide equal opportunities for all employees. An inclusive employer brand should communicate a message of belonging and respect for diversity to job candidates current, and former employees. This can be achieved through various channels, such as social media, job descriptions, company websites, and internal communications. Technology can play a vital role in creating and promoting an inclusive brand. Women are 16 percent less likely than men to apply to a job after viewing it, and women apply to 20 percent fewer jobs than men.[2] This has to do with the fact that women only apply for a job if they meet 100 percent of the qualification criteria, whereas men apply when they only meet 60 percent.[3] With technology, job posts can be optimized to appeal to a broader range of candidates and limit the number of candidates that self-select to not apply. This goes beyond limiting the qualification criteria; the algorithms are trained on large data sets and

Brand and Recruit

- Job post optimization
- AI-powered screening tools
- Blind hiring software
- (AI) skill assessments
- Recruitment analytics
- Talent and target audience insights and benchmarks

Onboard and Ramp up

- Talent insights
- Network analysis for onboarding and inclusion purposes

Learn and Develop

- Mixed reality for inclusive learning
- Immersive learning to reduce unconscious bias

Engage and Retain

- Performance technologies
- Pay equity analysis
- Organizational network analysis to detect diversity of networks

Offboard and Rehire

- Ethical decision making, especially when organizations are leveraging AI for offboarding purposes

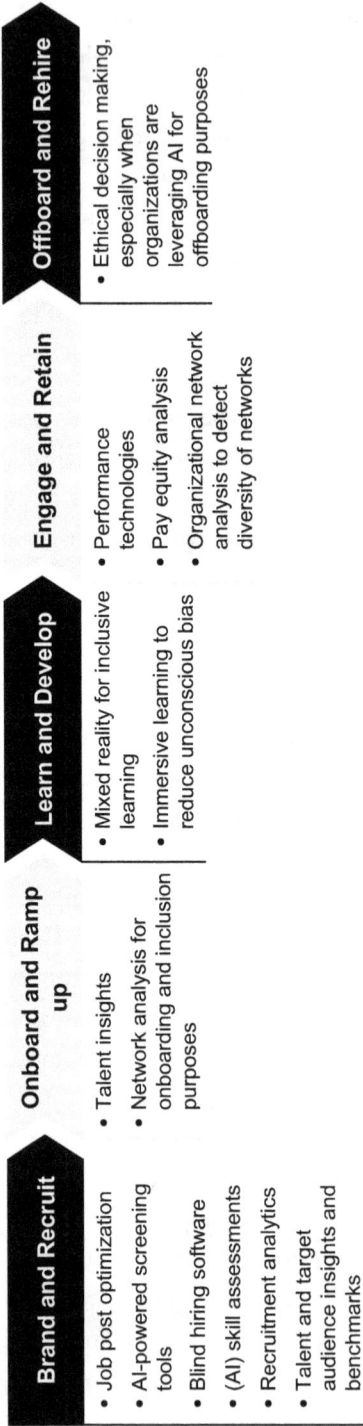

Figure 4.1 Technologies throughout the employee life cycle to support fairness at work

rewrite job applications or suggest changes in wording to better appeal to and resonate with different target audiences. Such approaches are often used not only for attracting more gender-diverse candidates, but also to attract candidates with different levels of education and from different social backgrounds. It can also help when organizations are hiring in multiple countries and cultures and writing job descriptions that are more appealing in different parts of the world.

To be more inclusive, organizations can also use technology to make their websites, vacancies, and digital content accessible to people with different abilities. This can include using alt-text for images or closed captioning for videos and ensuring that websites are designed with accessibility in mind.

Screening and Assessing

Being unbiased when screening or assessing candidates is essential for creating a fair, diverse, and inclusive work environment. It can help organizations attract the best candidates, avoid legal issues, and improve employee retention rates. There are several technologies that can help reduce bias when screening or assessing candidates.

- *AI-powered screening tools* can help remove unconscious bias from the screening process by eliminating demographic information from resumes and using algorithms to match job requirements with candidates' skills and experiences.
- *Blind hiring software* can remove all identifying information from resumes to ensure that recruiters focus solely on candidates' qualifications and skills.
- *Skill assessments* can be used to evaluate a candidate's abilities without relying on subjective assessments or biases.

Further recruitment tools that use data analytics can help reduce bias by identifying patterns or trends in the recruitment process that are associated with bias. This can help companies make data-driven decisions to improve their recruitment practices and create a more diverse and inclusive workforce.

Case: Data-Centric Fairness at the ANWB

Starting with an end goal in mind and building a strong foundation for a program are essentials that I recommend to my customers. However, I also recommend to not implement various kinds of technologies and programs all at once but rather to experiment and learn from outcomes. These are two points that were raised in my conversation with Albert Hoekstra, head of D&I at the ANWB.* Albert has built a foundational program that touches upon all facets of the employee life cycle. Within the program, targets are set by the business, which align with the foundational program, and as a result, HR instruments might require changes. These changes can be fueled by technology but are led by strategy. The ANWB is an organization with a variety of business units that greatly differ from one another. The types of challenges faced by D&I are also different in each unit. One thing that is already a core element in the ANWB's D&I strategy is data.

For recruiting, the ANWB looks at benchmark data to see if their employee database reflects society and the industry from a diversity perspective. This means that, overall, the ANWB strives to be a 50 percent male and 50 percent female organization, but if a business unit operates in a male- or female-dominated industry, targets are set accordingly. For example, the ANWB has a unit that employs car mechanics, which as a profession is still dominated by men. In 2019, CBS reported that in the Netherlands, only up to 2 percent of car mechanics were women.[4] As such, setting a target for hiring for 3 percent is already above the market average, and setting the target at 50 percent would be unrealistic. Another business unit operates in the travel industry, which mainly employs women. While many

---

* The Royal Dutch Tourist Association, ANWB, is an association that promotes the interests of its members in the field of mobility, holidays, and leisure with a unique mix of influencing and service-providing activities. In this work, the ANWB wants to contribute to the sustainable development of society. The ANWB employs 4.000 people. More at www.anwb.nl.

organizations focus on hiring and promoting more women, I found it interesting to see that the ANWB has a tailored strategy that really looks to reflect society. For example, in the travel unit, the ANWB is looking into how it can attract more men. Having this data helps not only to better understand the market and the target audience, but also to fuel a change in how branding campaigns are created to reach a wider audience.

Another analysis conducted by the ANWB is equal pay analysis. The data shows that there is no significant difference in pay and that it is equal. Albert mentioned that this can also be explained by the fact that the organization has many women in senior and management positions. The ANWB was able to attract many women to management positions because it allows management to work four days. Moreover, the salary scales are transparent, which promote equal compensation.

As more laws and mandates are being implemented by the government, I was curious about how Albert and his team are reporting on new requirements. He mentioned that they already log many data points in the applicant tracking system (ATS) and core HR systems to show that there is no discrimination and to be able to report on the government-set Key Performance Indicators (KPIs), such as those for equal pay and the percentage of women on management teams. The ANWB is developing another process to include in these systems to show that it has objectively assessed candidates. In addition, they have new processes in place that have replaced a single hiring manager with a selection committee.

Setting KPIs contributes to creating a more diverse organization, but creating a more inclusive organization requires other efforts as well. To create a more inclusive environment, the entire management took part in awareness training this year. This training leverages a variety of techniques, including gamified training to uncover bias and virtual reality (VR) to learn and understand how diverse employees experience work and life.

(*Continues*)

(Continued)

> The ANWB's top management is already quite diverse, and its CEO is a woman. From that perspective, the ANWB is already a market leader, but from other perspectives, there are still improvements to make. With the foundational program that Albert built and its implementation, he hopes that in the next few years, his role will be no longer necessary. This would be a great accomplishment because it would mean that D&I is embedded into the organization and management's goals, making a head of D&I position obsolete.

Interviewing

At my previous employers, I applied the Rooney rule[†] when selecting candidates to interview, to increase diversity in our hiring processes, and this rule is adopted by many other organizations. While there is not yet any specific technology that is used to enforce the Rooney rule, technology can help support and facilitate its implementation. Data can help with understanding the diversity of the target audience. For example, knowing that 20 percent of data scientists are female or 20 percent of data scientists are Black in a certain country or region is an insight that can help facilitate an equitable interview process. Furthermore, video interviewing platforms can help reduce bias by allowing candidates to answer prerecorded questions, ensuring that all candidates answer the same questions. Then, reviewing the answers by a diverse hiring panel can reduce bias. Some of these technologies allow anonymizing personal characteristics. For example, video interviewing platforms also allow anonymization features, such as the anonymization of a candidate's face, voice, and background, to ensure a fairer and unbiased evaluation. Online skills assessments measure candidates' abilities in various areas, and by focusing on specific skills rather than subjective traits, these assessments can help to remove biases from the hiring process. Some AI tools use natural language processing

---

[†] The Rooney rule is a policy that requires National Football League teams to interview minority candidates for head coaching and senior football operation positions. It was named after Dan Rooney.

to analyze and evaluate written responses from candidates. By removing identifying information and focusing on the content of the response, these tools can help reduce bias in the initial stages of the hiring process. In their blog post "How HR can tackle diversity using the Rooney Rule,"[5] Visier[‡] shares diversity metrics that support the Rooney rule initiative and how to measure these. The demographic metrics that matter are:

1. Who's getting interviewed?
2. Who's moving through each stage?
3. Who's doing the interviewing?
4. Who's getting hired?

In Figure 4.2, Visier visualizes the metrics of the interview process that can give insights to diverse candidates if the hiring process is friendly and where to make adjustments if the intended result is not met.

It is important to note that while these technologies can help in reducing biases and promote D&I in hiring, they are not foolproof.

Is our hiring process friendly to diverse candidates?

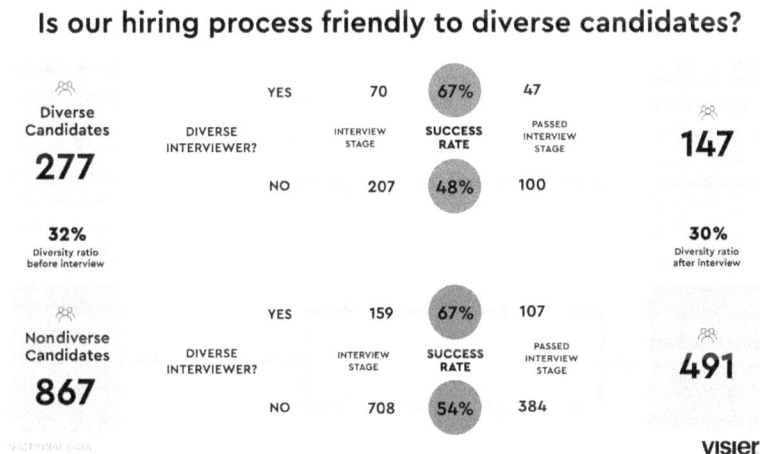

Figure 4.2 Illustrative metrics on hiring process, developed by Visier

‡ Visier is a global leader in people analytics and on-demand answers for people-powered business. Visier was founded in 2010 and headquartered in Vancouver, BC. Visier has 15,000 customers in 75 countries and employs around 600 employees in 7 office locations around the globe. More at www.visier.com.

Organizations must still be vigilant and conscious of their own biases when evaluating candidates.

Onboard and Ramp Up

A good onboarding process is critical for the success of a new hire and the overall success of an organization. A well-designed onboarding program can help new hires feel welcomed, supported, and engaged in their new roles. A comprehensive onboarding process can also help new hires understand their roles and responsibilities as well as their new organization's culture, values, and mission. This process can reduce the time it takes for new employees to become productive and start making meaningful contributions to the team. Data can show how well employees are onboarding. Having access to their new managers and other relevant people within the organization is crucial for their performance. It is important to understand when designing a fair onboarding process where the bias is in an organization. When I worked at Microsoft, after conducting an analysis, some of my customers found that male directors were more likely to spend time with male colleagues one level below them than with female colleagues one level below them and that female employees at the company had on average a smaller internal network size. If data shows that more women than men leave an organization with a shorter tenure, looking at relevant data to understand how much time is invested by the leadership could contribute to a longer tenure for a certain group of employees. Other metrics are included in Figure 4.3, which illustrates how networks can be analyzed using e-mail, calendar, and chat data. In particular, the figure examines two data points. The first is the average hours a new employee spends in manager one-on-one meetings[§] and if there is a difference in time spent between newly hired males and females and their managers. The second is the internal network size[**] of the newly

---

[§] A manager one-on-one meeting is a meeting between an employee and their direct manager.

[**] Internal network size is calculated based on the number of people within the company with whom a person has had at least two meaningful interactions within the last four weeks. More information can be found at https://learn.micosoft .com/en-us/viva/insights/use/metric-definitions.

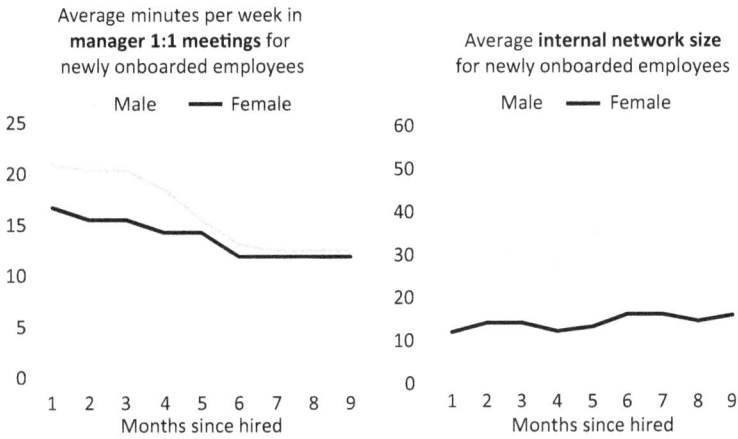

Figure 4.3 Illustrative onboarding example based on Microsoft Viva Insights data

hired employees. The example in Figure 4.3 shows that newly hired men receive more one-on-one time with their managers in the first four months of onboarding. Internal network growth also happens more quickly for newly onboarded males, which could be a consequence of more time spent with their managers. Having these insights as an organization and understanding potential correlations can help in effectively changing parts of the program.

In Figure 4.3, an analysis was conducted on gender, but of course if the data is available, this could also be done on other parameters within an organization.

Learn and Develop

Inclusivity in learning and development benefits everyone involved. It creates a more positive and engaging learning environment, promotes critical thinking and creativity, and prepares learners to work and interact with diverse groups of people. Recognizing that different learners have different learning styles and preferences ensures that organizations offer a variety of instructional methods and technologies. VR and augmented reality (AR) can simulate real-world environments and scenarios, making learning more engaging and interactive. They can also provide immersive experiences that cater to different learning styles and ambitions. AI can personalize learning experiences by analyzing learning data and providing customized recommendations based on learning preferences and abilities. AI can also provide real-time feedback and assessment, helping learners and their employers identify areas where they need to improve to be more inclusive.

To create a fairer working environment, trainings are designed to promote DEI in the workplace. The goal of these trainings is to create a work environment that is welcoming, supportive, and respectful to all employees, regardless of their background, identity, or abilities. DEI trainings typically cover a range of topics, such as those listed here.

- Employees are taught about the unconscious biases that we all possess, which can affect our perceptions and decision making. The training aims to help employees recognize their biases and learn strategies to overcome them.
- Employees are taught about different cultures and how to work effectively with people from diverse backgrounds. The training helps employees to understand and appreciate cultural differences and to avoid stereotypes and cultural misunderstandings.
- Employees are taught about microaggressions, which are subtle, often unintentional acts of discrimination that can harm marginalized groups. The training aims to help employees recognize microaggressions and learn strategies to avoid them.
- Employees are taught effective communications skills that can help build trust, understanding, and respect in the workplace. The training focuses on active listening, constructive feedback, and open dialogue.
- Managers and supervisors are taught about their role in creating an inclusive and equitable work environment. The training aims to help managers understand how their actions and decisions can impact their employees and to develop strategies for promoting DEI.

Case: Immersive Knowledge Transfer to Everyone

CoVince[††] is a company that fosters learning, collaboration, and community through a cutting-edge metaverse platform. The platform is designed to provide a stimulating and interactive environment that promotes creativity, innovation, and teamwork. The platform is optimized for learning and skills development. The platform offers parks and journeys with a variety of experience. It can be accessed through multiple devices and leverages immersive technologies, such as VR and AR, to create engaging and interactive experiences. The parks and journeys can take many forms, from educational games to training simulations, and they can be used for a wide range of learning purposes, including skills development, career training, and personal development. Users can interact with other employees, other learners from other companies, instructors, and digital content in a dynamic and engaging way, allowing for more immersive and effective learning experiences.

CoVince also offers Campus Parks, which are growth parks dedicated to offering learning experiences that support all didactic flows. They constitute a form of social learning that provides both communities and live classroom interactions. When I spoke with Richard van Tilborg and Melanie van Halteren, the platform's founders, they shared an interesting story of one of their clients, a university.

Part of a professor's job at a university is to transfer their knowledge to their students, but CoVince developed this training with a professor for immersive knowledge transfer in businesses, for example, for developing commercial leadership skills for young professionals and consultants. Neurological research shows how information

(*Continues*)

[††] CoVince designed a metaverse platform that forsters learning, collaboration, and community. More at https://connect.covince.com/www/english/About-Us .html.

(*Continued*)

is best remembered by its recipients, and this information can be used to develop teaching and speech skills for professors. Through a mixed-reality program, there are several modules that can be taught. The program collects all types of data, including about speech speed, intonation, gestures, and tone. Based on research and the data points, the program can prescribe what the learner needs to do differently in order to be more effective. This can be practiced in the program in many ways, for example, by adjusting only speech speed or a combination of speed and volume. The program can also offer simulations of teaching in a classroom, speaking at a large event, or presenting at a well-known talk show.

Most trainings are not developed for people with different abilities. The beauty of leveraging these technologies for learning and development is that it can also be used when, for example, someone is visually impaired. The training will still help the learner receive feedback on how to be better, while the impaired person can learn at their own pace, best suited to their own needs.

As the metaverse continues to evolve, I expect more growth parks and learning platforms to emerge, offering new opportunities for employees to learn, grow, and connect in virtual environments.

Immersive learning can be an effective way to address many of the topics covered in DEI training at work. It involves creating a simulated environment that mimics real-world scenarios, which can help employees to develop skills and knowledge in a more engaging and interactive way. For example, VR and AR can be used to simulate different cultural experiences, allowing employees to interact with people from different backgrounds and learn about different cultures. This can help employees to develop cultural competence and avoid stereotypes and cultural misunderstandings. Immersive learning can also be used to teach communication skills, such as active listening and open dialogue. Employees can participate in simulated conversations and scenarios that require them to practice these skills in a safe and controlled environment.

Combining different types of methodologies can provide a more comprehensive and effective approach to promoting DEI in the workplace.

Case: Reducing Microaggressions in the Workplace Through Immersive Learning Experiences

VR is being used at increasingly more organizations to help employees understand microaggressions and change their negative behaviors. On this topic, I spoke with Vivian Acquah, who is an inclusive workplace wellness advocate and a certified DEI consultant.[‡‡]

She and her organization have been using VR for the past 18 months to create immersive experiences to help organizations reduce microaggressions, biases, and other noninclusive behaviors at work. These experiences allow employees to experience exclusion in a safe way, and employees learn to understand what exclusion does on the individual and organizational levels. The immersive experience confronts employees with their own biases and intrinsically motivates them to change their related behaviors. Though after the immersive experience employees oftentimes feel inspired to change, the program requires employees to have an accountability partner. With this partner, the employee shares their intended behavior changes, and the partner holds the employee accountable and supports them by regularly discussing the intended behaviors and goals associated with these behaviors.

These trainings can be used to better understand behaviors and microaggressions associated with racism, ageism, sexism, and other forms of discrimination. However, these are tough scenarios to start with for organizations. Therefore, Vivian starts with a neurodiversity experience; this experience helps employees to gain more understanding about microaggressions and other behaviors that can hurt inclusion. The beauty of an immersive experience compared to other learnings is that it activates the fight or flight modus; the employee's whole body responds to the experience. The brain is tricked into thinking that the experience is real, which has a lasting effect. Employees cannot unlearn the experience, and that unique reaction can help in setting personalized next steps to reduce the biases of the employee.

[‡‡] Vivian Acquah is a Certified Diversity Executive. More information about her and her company can be found at https://amplifydei.com/.

Engage and Retain

Technology can help organizations to be more inclusive to engage and retain talent by providing employees with more flexibility, accessibility, and personalized experiences. This can lead to increased job satisfaction, improved performance, and a more diverse and inclusive workforce. DEI technologies can use AI, machine learning, and advanced analytics to create insights into different aspects of the employee life cycle. Leveraging these technologies can make the decision-making process less prone to human bias.

Performance Measurement

Employers can use technology to track employee performance in a transparent and objective way. This can help to ensure that promotions and bonuses are based on merit rather than subjective judgment. Research suggests that men and women are assessed very differently at work. Specifically, a new research from Stanford University's Clayman Institute for Gender Research has found that managers are significantly more likely to critique female employees for coming on too strongly, and their accomplishments are more likely than men's to be seen as the result of team rather than individual efforts.[6]

Pay Equity Analysis

A pay equity analysis is a process used to identify and address pay disparities between different groups of employees. Employers can use software to analyze employee compensation and identify potential pay disparities based on gender, race, or other factors. This can help to ensure that all employees are paid fairly for their work. When conducting a pay equity analysis, it is important to determine the scope of the analysis, including the groups of employees to be compared, the relevant job roles, and the time frame for the analysis. It is also important to control for relevant factors that may impact pay, such as job tenured, education, experience, and job performance. This can help to observe where pay disparities derive from.

Analyzing pay at a high level provides a broad perspective on compensation structures and allows for high-level comparisons and identification of potential pay disparities between different groups. It can also help identify overall trends, such as pay gaps or pay disparities among different departments. However, analyzing pay at one level might mask the more nuanced issues within subgroups or levels. It fails to capture potential pay inequities that could exist within different categories. Diving deeper and analyzing at a more granular level can reveal more detailed insights. This approach enables a more precise identification of pay disparities and inequities that may exist within seemingly homogeneous groups. Deeper analysis allows organizations to identify potential biases or inconsistencies in compensation practices that may have gone unnoticed in a broader analysis. This level of analysis provides a better understanding of the factors driving pay differences and helps develop targeted strategies to address any identified issues.

Pay equity solely at a company level can be misleading if it fails to consider the composition of different genders within specific job levels or roles. For example, at a company level, the average salaries of male and female employees might appear to be relatively equal. However, when conducting a deeper analysis by examining job levels or roles, the data shows that one gender is predominantly represented in junior roles, while the other gender occupies senior positions. This situation can mask underlying pay inequities and limit the accuracy of the initial conclusion of pay equity. Analyzing pay at a deeper layer requires more extensive data and resources. It may also increase the complexity of the analysis, making it more time consuming and challenging to interpret the results. After the analysis, it is important to develop a plan to address the pay disparities. This may be adjusting pay for affected employees, but can also be revising job requirements or evaluating processes and implementing new policies and procedures to promote pay equity.

Organizations can identify any systemic barriers that may limit the representation of one gender in senior roles. Organizations can review the job structures to ensure that it provides equal opportunities for career advancement and progression for all genders. To promote pay equity, organization can set up promotion and development programs; these may involve mentorship initiatives, visibility programs, or leadership trainings.

Continuous monitoring and updating of the pay equity analysis is needed to ensure that pay disparities are not reintroduced and to track progress toward pay equity. It is important to note that while technology can provide valuable support, it should complement a comprehensive strategy and be implemented alongside robust policies, training programs, and ongoing commitment from leadership and HR teams. The technology solutions should be aligned with the organization's specific needs, data privacy regulations, and considerations for maintaining fairness and equity throughout the process.

Career Development

Designing structured and transparent people processes ensures that outcomes are fair and that employees perceive them as such. When processes are not transparent, employees can get concerned that they might not fit or do not understand how to progress in their careers. Technology can be used to facilitate transparent communication between employees and management. This ensures that all employees have access to the same information and are kept up to date on company policies and procedures. Technology can be used to collect anonymous feedback from employees, which can help to identify potential issues related to fairness at work. For example, online surveys or feedback forms can collect feedback from employees on various aspects of the work environment, such as communication, recognition, and opportunities for growth. Strong peer relationships help employees to stay connected to their teams. Data analysis and particular ONAs can help detect the diversity of networks and if employees are isolated. Networks are critical to career development, and a study has shown that there is a difference between the networks of successful male and female leaders.[7]

Male leaders benefit not from the size of their networks, but from being central in their network. Whereas women also benefit from being central in their networks, for women to achieve an executive position with the highest level of authority and pay, they should also have an inner circle of close female contacts. To help female leaders develop their careers and enhance their inner circle of close female contacts, organizations can take several actions to be supportive. Figure 4.4

illustrates how female leaders can build this inner circle and increase their visibility within the organization.

- Mentors, coaches, and sponsors can introduce female leaders to their own networks and provide opportunities for connection with other influential individuals. Through these relationships, female leaders can expand their circle of close contacts, including other female leaders who can offer support, guidance, and collaboration. All three can play a different role and an easy way to explain this is that "a coach talks to you, a mentor talks with you, and a sponsor talks about you."[8] A mentor can help female leaders navigate the workplace culture and challenges, power dynamics, and relationships. A mentor can also provide guidance on longer-term career path goals and acts as a trusted advisor. Where a coach helps more to navigate the current job responsibilities and working through immediate challenges, sponsors help employees move up in their careers, provide access to key assignments, and speak on behalf of the other person behind closed doors. Sponsors use their influence to benefit the career from their protégé.
- Networking can be done externally and internally, sometimes through employee resources groups (ERGs). By participating in these events, female leaders can meet and establish connections with other professionals in their industry or field. These opportunities allow for the creation of relationships with other female leaders, fostering a support system and enabling the formation of an inner circle of close contacts.
- Leadership development programs tailored for female leaders often incorporate networking activities, collaborative projects, and group discussions. These programs provide an environment where female leaders can interact with their peers, share experiences, and develop relationships with like-minded individuals who can become part of their inner circle. These leadership programs often also offer internal mobility or promotion opportunities. When female leaders are provided

with fair and transparent opportunities for advancement within the organization, they have the chance to connect with colleagues across different levels and departments. As they progress in their careers, they are more likely to build relationships with other leaders, including female leaders, contributing to the formation of a close network.

A personal board can play a valuable role in enhancing the career of female leaders. It consists of a group of trusted individuals who provide guidance, support, and expertise to help employees navigate their professional journey. A personal board typically consists of individuals from different backgrounds, industries, and areas of expertise. They bring diverse perspectives and experiences, offering employees a well-rounded view of career decisions and challenges. Their collective insight can help employees gain insights and consider different approaches to achieve their career goals. A personal board can also hold the employee accountable for career goals and aspirations. Through regular "board" meetings and discussions, they can help the employee set goals, monitor progress, and provide support and motivation along the way.

Personally, I use my board when facing and making critical career decisions, for example, when I was making the decision to change industries or when I was deciding about taking on a new role. My board offered me valuable insights, challenged my assumptions, and helped me make strategic choices by also evaluating the potential risks and rewards of different options. Building a successful career can sometimes be challenging and overwhelming. A personal board can also offer emotional support during difficult times, providing encouragement, motivation, and a safe space to discuss concerns and fears. They can provide reassurance, boost confidence, and help employees overcome obstacles in their career path.

Figure 4.4 is specified to females because the research indicates that female leaders benefit from creating an inner circle of close female contacts. However, the model can also be applied to other (underrepresented) groups within an organization. Implementing the actions mentioned can also be facilitated by various technologies and platforms. When selecting technologies for helping female leaders or other minorities enhance their

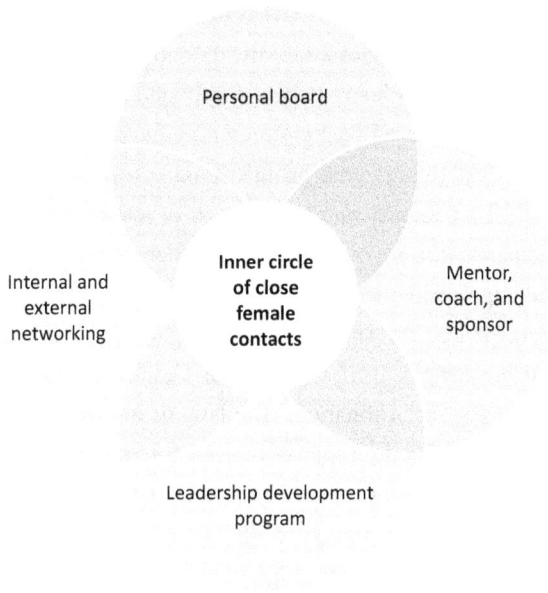

Personal board

Internal and
external
networking

**Inner circle
of close
female
contacts**

Mentor,
coach, and
sponsor

Leadership development
program

*Figure 4.4 Female leadership model to create an inner circle of close
female contacts*

careers, it is, like with the other processes, essential to consider factors
such as ease of use, data security, integration capabilities with existing
systems, and the specific requirements of the organization's initiatives.
Additionally, the chosen technologies should align with the organization's
policies and comply with privacy and data protection regulations.

Offboard and Rehire

There are a variety of policies to protect employees and to prevent organizations from discrimination. In my own country, the Netherlands, we
have a policy that in the event of layoffs for economic reasons, a propor-
tionality principle determines the order of dismissals. This means that the
age structure within an organization will remain the same as much as possible before and after the restructuring, protecting employees from being
discriminated based on age. However, there is no protection in this law
for other underrepresented groups. Moreover, oftentimes, the data of the
representation of different groups within an organization before and after

layoffs is not shared, which can have a big impact. For example, at the end of 2022 and beginning of 2023, the technology industry announced massive layoffs.[9] In an industry largely dominated by one group, employees from underrepresented backgrounds may have to bear the brunt of these layoffs. Underrepresented groups inhabit relatively more roles in nontechnical departments, such as business development or marketing, and these departments are oftentimes hit harder than the product development and engineering departments.

In December 2022, a lawsuit was filed against Twitter, accusing the company of violating federal and state of California laws by committing workplace sex discrimination. The lawsuit alleges that Twitter laid off 57 percent of its female employees compared to 47 percent of its male employees. In engineering roles, the lawsuit claims that 63 percent of women lost their jobs compared to 48 percent of men. In addition to laying off a statistically significant higher proportion of women than men, there were also a number of policies implemented that could have a disproportionate impact on women, such as expectations to work unreasonable hours and employees being required to work in physical offices.[10]

Rather than a traditional approach, the leadership needs to take a holistic look at how proposed cuts will affect their workforce prior to committing to layoffs. To avoid disproportionately affecting underrepresented groups in the workplace and negatively impacting the employee experience, doing a data analysis before and after laying off employees to make sure that the impact on certain groups is limited is beneficial to employees, especially the ones staying at the organization.

Ethics

It is important that HR professionals have the time and opportunity to discover what really matters to employees and that they have the courage to continue to look at the organization from different values of employees in order to contribute to an inclusive work environment. In doing so, it is necessary to constantly balance between the perspectives of the organization, the team, and the individual employee to enable both the employee and the organization to thrive. When organizations invest more in technologies and data solutions to understand the behavior of their employees, it is very important for the leadership and HR teams to think and act ethically and fairly. Before starting to collect and analyze sensitive data, a clear plan is needed, and employees need to be able to understand from where the data derives and what the possible actions would be, based on the potential findings.

AI tools help millions of people around the world, but oftentimes when employees start using a tool, they do not get trained on how to properly use it or receive guidelines for its ethical use. For example, ChatGPT,§§ which became a very popular tool during the authoring of this book, has the ability to generate conversational texts, but concerns are that it could generate fake news or other misleading content. The tool is based on billions of words and a large data set. However, it is not known what specific data is used to train the model, and it is entirely unregulated, which means that biased data could inform its modeling. Using ChatGPT can have severe consequences, such as the spread of false information or even the propagation of hatred. The risk of uploading confidential information in ChatGPT or similar tools is the potential compromise of sensitive data, as these platforms operate in cloud environments and may not guarantee the same level of security as inhouse systems. As an organization, when employees are using such tools, it is important to think about what guardrails are put in place to prevent augmentations of existing inequalities. The more these tools are being made generally available, the more important it is that the organization's ethical behaviors, in line with the companies values, are being modeled by employees.

Employees are using AI tools on a daily basis, often without their employer's knowledge. They use a range of tools, from those that reduce background noise during calls to tools that design content in a flash or tools that write high-performing cold e-mails at scale. As employees will work increasingly more with these tools, it is important to understand the limitations of these technologies and to know which tool can be used

---

§§ ChatGPT is part of OpenAI and is still in research preview. In the first half of 2023, the tool is being offered for free to receive feedback from users in order to learn about the model's strengths and weaknesses. Learn more at chat.openai .com.

for what purpose. In Chapter 1, I write not only that employees need to digitally upskill because of all the tools currently entering the workforce, but also that employees need ethical skills. If an employee leverages an openAI to create a whitepaper for a customer, the benefits are obvious. AI bots can write the paper faster and potentially more accurately. However, the AI bot does not (yet) use proper references, which can mean that when employees do not check the text to understand the research behind the AI bot, they potentially expose themselves or even their organization to litigation by not honoring the authors' rights.

Another thing to be considered is that when an organization is leveraging machine learning on employee data, one must make sure that the data is sufficient and significantly relevant and ethical. Do employees know that their data is being used and for what purpose? Do managers know when a recommendation is being done, what data is being used, how the model works, and how that leads to the recommendation? Leaders need to continue to question if the right thing has been done and for the right reasons.

Conclusion

DEI is a topic that is talked about a lot. Josh Bersin's Elevating Equity Research[11] report finds that determining how to achieve DEI is an unsolved problem in business, and despite years of effort, most companies see achieving DEI as a work in progress. Despite the hard work by DEI leaders and many CHROs, only 20 percent of companies hold themselves fully accountable for inclusion and diversity, and 40 percent see it as a compliance issue to avoid legal, reputational, or compliance risks.[12]

Technology can play a significant role in creating a more equitable workplace by providing tools and solutions that address various aspects of DEI and accessibility throughout the entire employee life cycle. Immersive learning can reduce biases and microaggressions in the workplace, where analytics can provide organizations insights into how to create a more equitable and fair organization. While technologies and analyses can be a powerful enabler, it is essential to ensure that its implementation is done with careful consideration for biases and inclusivity. Diversity by design is therefore advised, next to ongoing assessments, regular training, and evaluations of the technology. These are all crucial to mitigate unintended negative consequences and promote a truly equitable and inclusive work environment.

The use of AI tools at work can bring numerous benefits, such as increased efficiency and accuracy in decision making. However, as these tools become more prevalent in the workplace, it is important to ensure that they are being used fairly and without bias. This requires careful consideration of the design and implementation of AI tools, as well as ongoing monitoring and evaluation to identify and address any issues that may arise. Not only is fairness in the use of AI tools at work important from ethical and moral standpoints, but it also helps to create a more inclusive and diverse workplace where all employees have an equal opportunity for success. By prioritizing fairness in the use of AI tools, organizations can unlock the full potential of these technologies while also promoting a more just and equitable society.

CHAPTER 5

People Analytics

The world of work has been changing for decades, and it has become harder to become and stay a market or industry leader. People matter more than ever, and there is an exponential payoff for building and maintaining high-performing teams, as the top companies make more profit per worker than their competitors. Whereas business models and even products can be replicated, one of the main determining factors that cannot be copied is people.

Organizations do realize that their employees are their human capital but struggle to understand what their employees do and what actions facilitate their employees to thrive. This is particularly true for information workers, who are critical to any organization's effort to transform culture and change behavior for two reasons.

1. Information workers often constitute an organization's most highly skilled resource, as they perform critical functions. They are also often an organization's most expensive group of workers.
2. Over the past 30 years, growth in most work categories has either significantly slowed or stagnated. Knowledge work, however, continues to grow and is becoming an increasingly important aspect of our economy.[1]

Employers have insights into the daily operations of frontline workers, but it is often difficult to understand what information workers do and where they add value. This group is grossly underrepresented when it comes to analytics, because their cognitive, nonroutine work is by nature difficult to measure. Without the ability to quantify the success of information workers, an organization has to rely on intuition, practical wisdom, and corporate lore to identify the behaviors that correlate with their success.

People analytics can help companies measure the success of information workers, and as such, many studies agree that people analytics are top of mind for increasingly more companies. Many organizations will use forms of behavioral economics and AI- or machine learning (ML)-driven insights to nudge employees' actions. The increased interest in people analytics in recent years is partly due to technological developments, the availability of open source (or freely available) software to perform advanced analyses, and the increasing trend toward evidence-based HR policy. Insight222's People Analytics Trends 2021 research shows the degree to which organizations realize the value of people analytics teams. For example, in 2021, for every 2,900 employees in an organization, there was 1 person in charge of people analytics, compared to a 4,000:1 ratio in the previous year, which reflects an increased interest in people analytics.[2]

However, using an organization's own data in policy development or people analytics, is still a major challenge for HR. It has taken HR departments longer than many other organizational departments, such as marketing and logistics, to understand data and analytics. The effective use of people analytics can be very valuable for HR, because general insights from research and other information sources can be made suitable for and applicable to their own organization. People analytics can also help the HR department to test its own effectiveness in responding better and faster to developments in the labor market and other external developments, and to base decision making more on evidence and less on gut feelings. In other words, utilizing people analytics makes HR tangible, visible, and agile.

What Is People Analytics?

People analytics is the use of data to understand and manage a workforce. This can include analyzing data on employee performance, turnover, engagement, and other workforce-related metrics. People analytics can also be referred to as workforce analytics, HR analytics, or workforce intelligence. The goal of people analytics is to improve decision making and strategic planning in areas such as talent management, recruitment, and employee development and to improve business performance. People analytics is not the simple implementation of a digital system or a HR information system. It is part of a strategy, an organizational change, and an overall digital and cultural transformation. An organization that makes effective use of people analytics has a different view on the use of internal HR data than an organization that only wants to perform several analyses on data.

People analytics can be used to identify patterns and trends in the workforce that can inform decisions related to hiring, promotions, and performance management. It can also be used to identify areas where an organization is underperforming and to develop strategies for improvement. Additionally, people analytics can help organizations to identify and address issues related to employee engagement and retention. Beneficial not only for an employer but also especially for employees, people analytics can also be used to create a more inclusive work environment and better well-being for workers.

Data used in people analytics can come from a variety of sources, such as core HR systems, collaboration technologies, time-tracking software, employee surveys, and social media. Figure 5.1 illustrates technologies that can be used as sources for analysis.

The data is then analyzed using techniques, such as statistical analysis, machine learning, and data visualization. Oftentimes, the terms used are descriptive, diagnostic, predictive, and prescriptive data points.

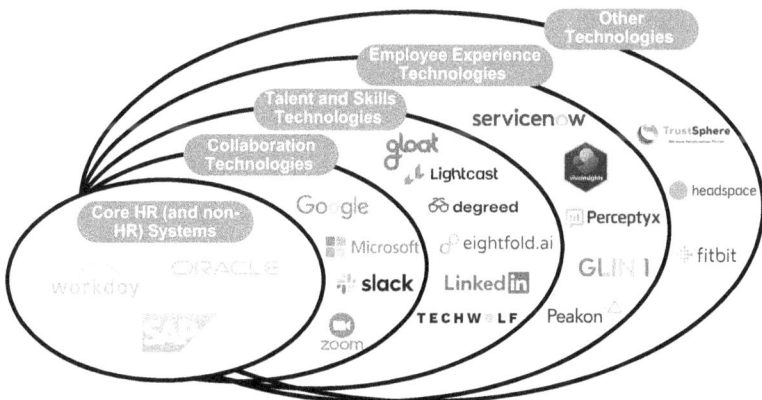

Figure 5.1 *Illustrative example of technologies that can be used for people analytics*

Descriptive Analytics

Descriptive analytics is a type of data analysis that focuses on summarizing and presenting historical data in a way that describes past trends, patterns, and insights.

Descriptive analytics is often the first step in the data analysis process, as it provides the foundation for further analysis and decision making. By examining past trends and patterns, organizations can identify areas for improvement and make better-informed decisions about future strategies and actions.

Descriptive data is often being used to understand historical data and to identify patterns and trends that can inform decision making. It involves the collection, analysis, and interpretation of data on employees, such as demographic information, job performance, and engagement levels. In people analytics, descriptive analytics helps to visualize the behavior of employees and give insights into these behaviors to be used by various groups.

The goal of descriptive people analytics is to understand the characteristics and behavior of the workforce and to identify patterns and trends that can inform decision making related to human resources, such as recruiting, training, and retention. Descriptive people analytics can be used to identify areas of strengths and weaknesses within the workforce and to develop strategies to improve employee engagement, productivity, well-being, and overall employee experience. Interesting analyses are inflow and outflow, age ratio, male–female ratio, fixed–flex ratio, number of years of service, reason for outflow, and expected outflow in connection with reaching retirement age. Analyses vary between organizations and even between business units, and it is wise to set up a steering group or management committee to learn whether or not there are certain hypotheses or expectations that need to be tested.

Diagnostic Analytics

Diagnostic analytics is a type of data analysis that focuses on the root causes of a particular problem or issue. It involves examining data to understand what factors contributed to a particular outcome and why it occurred. Diagnostic analytics is often used in conjunction with descriptive analytics, which provides a summary of historical data, to gain a deeper understanding of the data and its underlying causes. Some common techniques used in diagnostic analytics include data mining, statistical analysis, and root cause analysis. Diagnostic analytics can be a powerful tool for people analytics, helping organizations to identify the underlying factors that are contributing to particular patterns or trends in employee behavior or performance.

By understanding the root cause of issues such as low productivity, high turnover, or poor employee engagement, organizations can develop targeted strategies to address these issues and create a more positive and productive workplace. For example, if an organization is experiencing high turnover rates, diagnostic analytics might be used to identify the underlying factors that are contributing to this trend. This process could involve analyzing data on employee demographics, job satisfaction, compensation, and other relevant factors to identify the root causes of the turnover. Once these factors have been identified, the organization can develop targeted strategies to address them, such as improving employee benefits, increasing job satisfaction, or providing more opportunities for career development and advancement.

The goals of diagnostic analytics in people analytics are to use data to gain insights into employee behavior and performance and to develop strategies to improve organizational effectiveness and achieve business objectives.

Predictive Analytics

Predictive intelligence tells us what is going to happen. Predictive people analytics is the application of predictive modeling and analytics to data related to HR and the workforce of an organization. It involves the use of statistical and ML techniques to analyze and make predictions about future workforce trends and patterns, such as employee turnover, performance, engagement, potential burnout, or other well-being challenges.

The goal is to use data and analysis to anticipate future events and to proactively make decisions that will positively impact an organization and its workforce. Examples of predictive analytics include using data on past employee performance and demographic information to predict which new hires are most likely to be successful, or using data on employee engagement and demographic information to predict which employees are most likely to leave a company. Predictive analytics is a powerful tool for HR and business leaders to make data-driven decisions that can improve workforce productivity, reduce costs, increase organizational performance, and create a better employee experience.

Predictive analytics is also being used for strategic workforce planning where the analysis of a current workforce can be carried out in advance. This creates data on how the workforce will develop if the personnel policy remains unchanged. However, be careful when making statements based on data from the past: while the data can give a good indication of a trend, it is often insufficient for making reliable predictions. For example, with the nature of jobs changing with the advent of technology and AI, past data won't include these new trends when it comes to prediction. Some technologies offer predictive scenario planning that takes a forward looking approach that helps organizations anticipate future conditions, make informed decisions, and implement strategies that enhance their resilience and competitiveness in a rapidly changing world of work. Overall, the data needs to be sufficient to do an actual accurate prediction. Moreover, it is always wise to involve someone who understands data analysis. If HR personnel themselves do not have the necessary knowledge and skills, colleagues from, for example, finance, marketing, business intelligence, or external parties can often offer solutions.

Prescriptive Analytics

Prescriptive intelligence tells us what should be done. Prescriptive people analytics is a method of using data and analytics to make informed recommendations for improving an organization's HR practices and strategies. It involves collecting and analyzing data on employee behavior, performance, and engagement and using that information to identify areas of improvement and propose specific actions to address them.

The goal of prescriptive analytics is to improve organizational performance by effectively managing and developing employees. Prescriptive people analytics became increasingly used when workers began going back to the office and organizations started developing hybrid work schemes. Prescriptive analytics can be used, for example, for workspace optimization, work schedule optimization, or resources allocation. By analyzing historical data on office space utilization, employee schedules, project timelines, resource availability, time zone differences, employee availability and collaboration patterns, organizations can determine the number of desks or meeting rooms required or what teams could sit best on the same office floor. It can also help to identify which tasks or projects are better suited for remote work and which require in-person collaboration, helping organizations allocate resources and office space accordingly.

Prescriptive analytics could also be used to identify and address turn-over-related issues. By analyzing data on employee turnover rates, an organization can identify which departments or job roles have the highest turnover and then propose specific actions to address the issue, such as offering more training or career development opportunities for employees in those roles. It could also be used to improve performance management. By analyzing data on employee performance and engagement, an organization can identify which employees are most at risk of underperforming and then propose specific actions to support them, such as providing additional coaching and mentoring.

It is important to remember that people data analytics, although an effective tool for managing the workforce, should be used in conjunction with other methods, such as employee feedback and manager observations. By using people data analytics in conjunction with other methods, organizations can achieve a more comprehensive, accurate, and ethical understanding of their workforce. It allows for a deeper interpretation of data, validations of insights, consideration of individual experiences, and an ethical approach to decision making, ultimately leading to more effective and people-centric strategies. In addition, it is also important to ensure that any data collected is used in a fair and unbiased way and that appropriate safeguards are in place to protect employees' privacy and personal data.

Reaching Transformational Results

The topic of return on investment (ROI) always comes up when I discuss people analytics with my customers. It is interesting that while many organizations expect that the harder the analysis the stronger the impact, unfortunately this is not necessarily true. Figure 5.2—the people analytics maturity curve from PwC's report "Creating more value with your people analytics efforts"[3]—shows the difference between expected value and realized value.

Many organizations also do not know where to start or think that it has to be a linear process. The PwC report also states that organizations can already start with one single-use case, which could be a predictive, descriptive, or prescriptive one. However, in reality, what I have seen is that many organizations do start with descriptive and diagnostic analytics and that those skills are present in their HR departments. When analytics and modeling become more sophisticated, different types of skills are needed, and oftentimes, they do not reside within the HR department. This requires organizations to cross-collaborate or to find expertise outside of the company. When investing in a more sophisticated analysis, it is important to understand how this aligns with the business and what added value is expected.

Figure 5.3 shows the questions that are important to be able to answer before starting the analysis. First of all, it is important to understand what an organization is trying to achieve, who owns the problem, and what success would look like for the organization. It is also important to understand the level of transformation the organization is aiming to undergo, and if there is already a change program in place within the organization or if such a program will need to be established. People analytics can inform the transformation, but it is important that stakeholders are in agreement about what to do with the outcomes of the analysis and how the adoption and change program will be received and implemented within the organization.

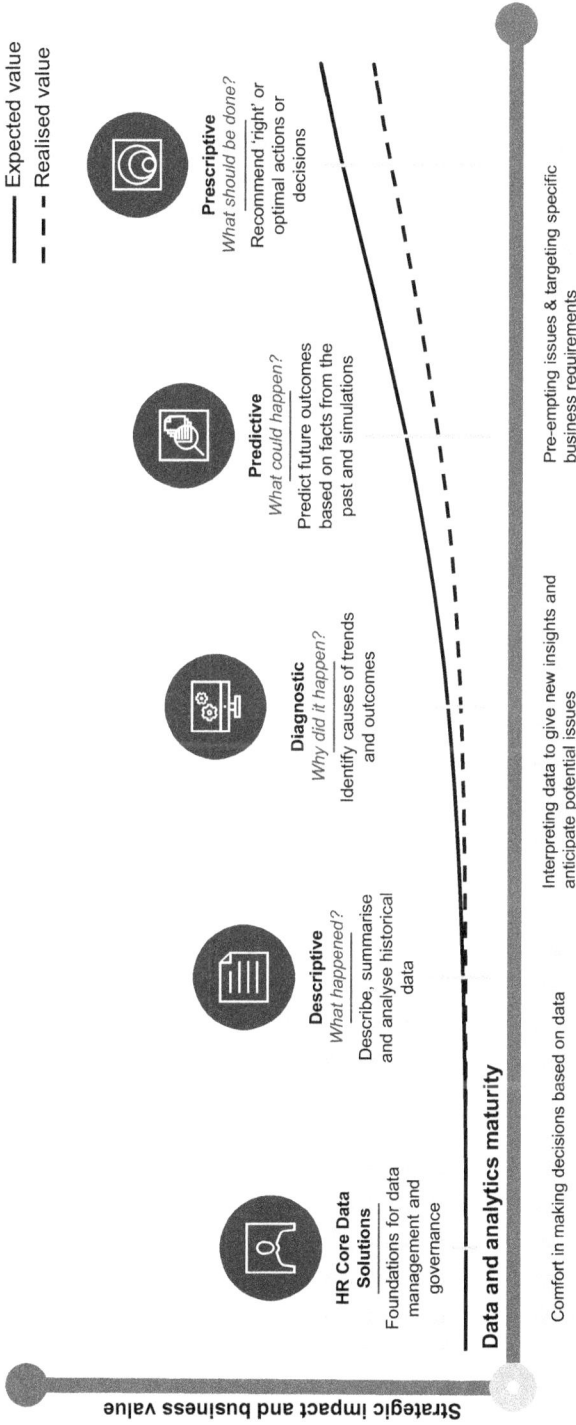

Figure 5.2 The people analytics maturity curve, developed by PwC

Business needs

1 What do we aspire to achieve?

2 What is the problem?

3 Who owns the problem?

4 What does success look like?

5 How does that help our business?

6 Does it create savings?

7 Does it produce better outcomes?

8 Does it increase the quality?

9 Does it delight our customer?

Business transformation

1 Is there already a change underway?

2 What will we do with our understanding?

3 What resources will be required to make the change?

4 What would increase the likelihood of the change being successful?

5 What would we like to do less or more of?

Hypotheses

1 Phase I (What can we tackle first?)

Your questions or hypothesis here

2 Phase II (What comes next?)

Your questions or hypothesis here

3 Phase III (Where do we aspire to go?)

Your questions or hypothesis here

Analysis scope and supporting data needed

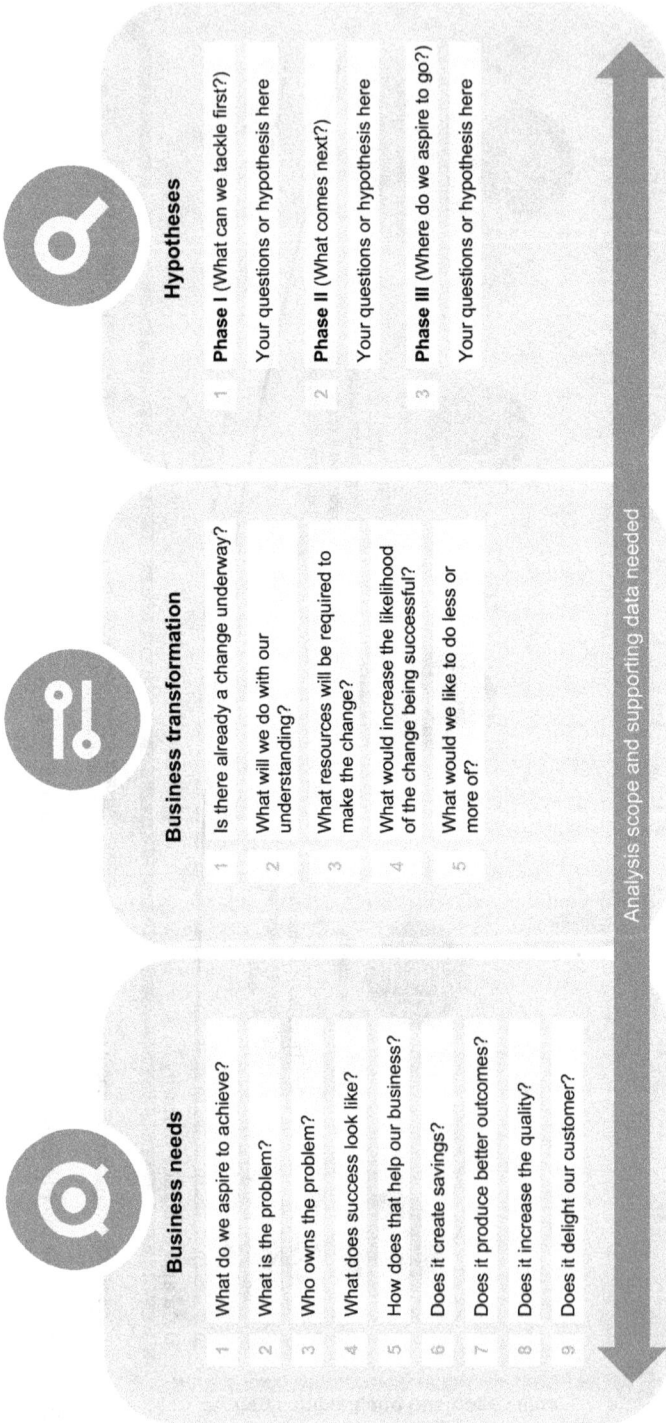

Figure 5.3 How to start a people analytics use case

Business needs are often focused on either reducing inefficiencies and costs or increasing productivity and revenues. For example:

- *Collaboration overload*: An analysis done by many of my customers. It helps them understand what happened in their organizations and why. These descriptive and diagnostic analyses give information on what inefficiencies exist regarding the collaboration between and within teams and how productivity can be increased. For example, it can indicate if employees have enough time during the day to get their work done. If all the time of an employee is spent in sending and reading e-mails and in meetings, there won't be time left to perform tasks. Two-hour blocks of uninterrupted time are critical for a person to be able to focus and complete critical individual work. When I was working at Microsoft, we found that individual contributors had around 15 hours of focus time per week compared to 10 hours for managers.[4] If employees don't have enough time to focus, this can lead to poor collaboration behaviors, such as multitasking during meetings.
- *Top performer behavior*: Where organizations can not only understand what top performers do differently but also prescribe how others should behave in order to reach similar results. These types of analyses contribute to increased productivity and revenues. For example, to close the gaps to help weaker performers to operate more like high performers is a way to drive additional revenue growth. To learn what top sales reps do differently, data analytics can help by mining behavioral data, such as number of meetings with clients, time spent with clients, and breadth and depth of internal and external networks from sales employees. This data can help to identify patterns in won and lost deals and generate insights into which behaviors drive wins and boost customer satisfaction.
- *Organizational design*: The spans (the number of direct reports a manager has) and layers (how many levels of management

the organizations has) in organizations and the number of roles can result in inefficiencies and loss of productivity. For example, when an employee becomes a manager and only has one or two direct reports, they still need to attend all the managers' meetings, which result in extra time spent but not necessarily extra impact delivered for their organization. Understanding the optimum for spans and layers within an organization is also a way of increasing productivity.

With my customers, I have looked at the three phases shown in Figure 5.3. While Phase III is important to understand where an organization aspires to go, phases I and II are the building blocks that work toward the aspirational future of the organization. Changing all workforce and human behaviors does require a lot of effort, and I do recommend to start with smaller experiments before scaling through an entire organization. Through experimentation, organizations can gain a deeper understanding of how different factors affect employee behavior and performance and use this knowledge to design more effective HR policies and practices that drive better business results.

Furthermore, by continuously experimenting and refining the approach, organizations can ensure that their people analytics initiatives remain relevant and impactful in a rapidly changing business environment. At a people analytics event, I met a director of people data science and employee insights at a large multinational. He is a fellow advocate for testing many hypotheses. In his presentation, he shared how his preferred method is using a contrarian view. This means prioritize long-term relevance of data sets over the focus on specific use cases. Instead of delivering projects end to end and being project focused, when having a contrarian view, the team is entity-centered and connects diverse data sets to address many hypotheses. When teams act in a contrarian view, they act more proactive and focus on moving fast, beyond the current priorities.

The contrarian view allows for running a pilot project to demonstrate the potential of people analytics in the restructuring process. It identifies a specific department or team within the organization that can serve as a test case. The pilot project serves as a tangible example to showcase the power of people analytics and how these insights can minimize the negative effects on employee morale or engagement. In a contrarian view, teams initiate open, transparent discussions to address concerns, answer questions, and actively engage with stakeholders. This allows to foster a culture of continuous improvement and innovation within the organization. In a pilot, the result can also be that the outcome of the analyses does not support the hypotheses and, if still in pilot phase, it is easier to pivot or to start working on supporting other hypotheses where a bigger organizational impact can be driven.

People Analytics Risks

Though I am a fan of people analytics, it is crucial as an organization to communicate transparently about the purposes of using an employee's data and to consider the potential risks for both the employee and the employer. Employees may be uncomfortable with the amount of personal data being collected about them and the potential for that data to be used in ways with which they do not agree. Employers can be held liable if they mishandle employee data resulting in a data breach or other privacy violations. If data is not collected or used in compliance with relevant laws and regulations, it can expose the organization to legal risks, such as discrimination lawsuits.

People analytics could perpetuate existing biases in the workforce if the data used to make decisions is not collected or analyzed properly. Where people analytics can be used to increase engagement, it can also have a negative impact on employee morale and engagement. If employees feel that their privacy is being violated, that their employers do not trust them or value their contributions, or that they are constantly being monitored and evaluated, it can lead to a decreased job satisfaction and engagement. The use of people analytics can aid in layoffs and other cost-cutting measures that can have a negative impact on employees. Without proper data governance, it can be difficult to ensure that the data is accurate and that any insights derived from it are reliable. It is unlikely that organizations will be able to get all the data reflecting their employees' behaviors and motivations. It's important for organizations to acknowledge the limitations of data availability and actively work toward mitigating biases and filling gaps in their understanding of employee behaviors. By employing a combination of data integration, representative sampling, qualitative research, expert insights, collaboration, and continuous improvement, organizations can make more informed decisions, reduce the risk of biases, and better address the nuances associated with employee behaviors. Many tools make data available for not only leaders but also managers to gain more insightful data of the daily operations of their teams. This democratization of data calls for the need of proper training. The degree of trust that you can put in the data depends on the size of the data set that is available for input. If a data set is too small, then correlations might not be significant. However, not learning how to question the data and taking it at face value can affect managers' ability to leverage these data points when making decisions.

It can be illegal for organizations to continuously collect data within a business intelligence system without sharing the purpose of the data collection. Due to the nature of the employee–employer relationship, it can be difficult for an employee to *not* consent to sharing all their data, as doing so can put them at risk of retaliation. In many countries, the law has not caught up with technologies, which makes it hard to interpret what constitutes employees' and employers' rights. In addition to observing the General Data Protection Ruling (GDPR), some countries do have laws to help employees be better protected. Moreover, as the use of data analytics and accordingly people analytics evolve, more rules and regulations are being developed as guidelines for workers councils. I encourage organizations that are implementing people analytics to act transparently by creating a clear communication and adoption strategy and clear guidelines and training processes for managers on how to work with this data to mitigate risks.

It is important for organizations to ensure that they are transparent about their use of people analytics. They should also ensure that any data collected is used in a fair and unbiased way and that appropriate safeguards are in place to protect employees' privacy and personal data. Additionally, organizations should have a good data governance plan in place to ensure that data is accurate and reliable.

People Analytics Example Analyses

Popular Types of Analyses That Use Both Active and Passive Data

Active and passive data are both commonly used in people analytics. Active data refers to data that is intentionally provided by individuals, such as survey results or performance metrics. This type of data is often collected through formal channels, such as interviews, questionnaires, or assessments.

Passive data, on the other hand, refers to data that is collected without an individual actively providing it. This type of data is often collected through digital sources, such as e-mail activity, calendar data, or social media posts. It can also be collected by observing employee attendance through the use of their keycards, telemetry data, or tracking sales metrics.

Both types of data are important in people analytics and can be used to gain insights into various aspects of employee behavior and performance. However, passive data is often considered to be more objective and less prone to bias, as it is collected automatically without the individual's input.

Surveys

A popular data source in people analytics is still the survey. Surveys can be used to gather data on a wide range of topics, such as employee engagement, satisfaction, and job performance. A good example of the application of a survey within an organization is an annual or biannual employee engagement survey that many organizations implement to gain insights into the engagement levels of employees across the organization. An exit interview is also a known survey type, used to gain more insights into why employees leave an organization, whose data can be used for developing improvement programs. Interviews with employees and managers, one on one or in a focus group, can provide more in-depth information on specific topics, such as specific challenges faced by a workforce or the effectiveness of current management practices.

A combination of both active survey data and passive behavioral data can provide many more insights, for example, when examining what differentiating factors exist between employees who are experiencing stress and employees who are thriving. Oftentimes, my customers think that the amount of hours (including overtime and/or weekend hours) that employees work directly correlates to the degree of stress they experience.

Figure 5.4 shows the outcome of an example analysis of active and passive data. The engagement survey's questions were on well-being, engagement, and work–life balance. The passive data includes overtime hours, weekend hours, the amount of time that employees require to focus and complete their work, the number of connections within their organization, and the amount of time spent with their manager. These groups were classified into four categories, where the overworked and involved categories of employees were often those who worked a similar amount of overtime or weekend hours. However, a differentiating factor was that employees that felt overworked generally spent less time with their managers or had a smaller internal network than those who did not feel overworked. The detached and underutilized groups both collaborated less than the other two groups. Intervention plans can be made to move the underutilized to the involved group, for example, by setting up a connection or virtual coffee program to enable employees to become

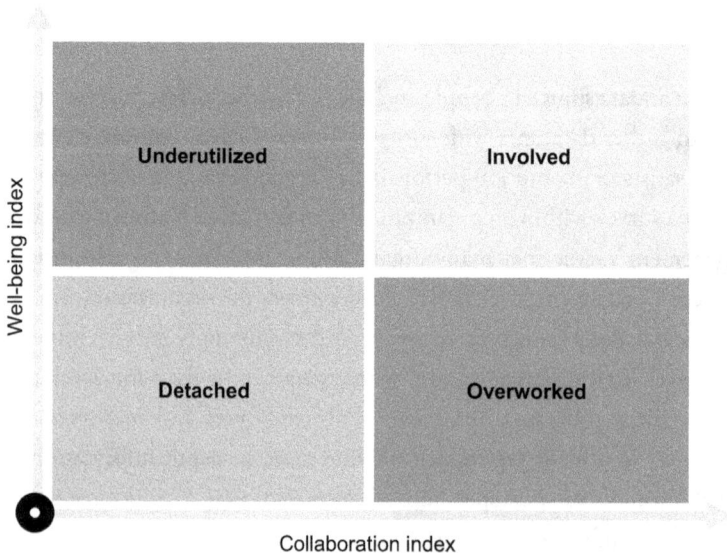

Figure 5.4 Four types of employees based on the well-being and collaboration indexes

better connected across the organization and build a wider network. The detached group not only rarely collaborates but also does not feel engaged. Overall, this group runs the risk of becoming overworked, and a deeper analysis on this group to understand other correlations that influence these behaviors needs to be done. Understanding how employees feel and the differences in their behaviors can help organizations establish different types of intervention plans for each of these groups.

This tailored approach contributes more to the needs of each group. Where, after the COVID-19 pandemic, organizations started to give their employees extra vacation or well-being days to recover, these were often not taken by employees, and a few extra vacation days do not necessarily solve the continuous stress that employees experience.[5] By understanding the impact of different types of behaviors, tailormade intervention plans can cause employees to feel overworked than to feel involved and thus drive a larger impact on the organization.

Organizational Network Analysis

Organizational network analysis (ONA) is a method of studying the relationships and communication patterns within an organization. It uses social network analysis techniques to map and analyze the connections between individuals, groups, and departments within an organization.

ONA can be used to study a variety of aspects of organizational life. For example, ONA can be used to identify who talks to whom, how often, and about what, which can help organizations understand their internal information flow and identify potential bottlenecks. ONA can also be used to map the informal networks, relationships, and connections that exist within an organization. Understanding these networks may be critical for understanding how work is done and how groups are influenced; this may not be captured by formal organizational structures. ONA can also be used to identify key players within an organization, such as those who are central to the flow of information or who have a high degree of influence over others.

ONA can be both active data, which is self-reported data from employees who are surveyed about their interactions and relationships, and passive data, which is system reported and measures interactions through other available data such as e-mail or meeting data. Self-reported data is very time intensive and frequently incomplete. Survey data is collected at one specific moment in time, whereas passive data can be collected continuously. The fact that survey data is collected at one point in time can lead to availability heuristic bias,[6] which occurs when people overestimate the likelihood of events based on how easily they can recall them from memory. For example, availability heuristic bias occurs when an employee is questioned about their network and shares the names of the people with whom they have most recently worked, because they think of them first. When analyzing passive data, it is not about what employees remember. Rather, it is the data that shows who actually collaborates with whom over a longer period of time. Since the data points are limited when using surveys, they have a faster computation time and lower computation costs. On the other hand, system-reported data does not require anything from an employee, because the data is automatically created by employees' everyday work. The missing data is often minimal, is not limited to one static point in time, can actually change over time, and can be updated at regular intervals. This makes it easier to understand the effects of interventions carried out by the organization. However, the computation of such data costs much more and takes longer, because the data set is much larger.

ONA can be used for different purposes, and its algorithms can measure different parameters.

Network Size

Network size is a basic measure used in ONA to describe the overall size of a network. It refers to the total number of individuals or nodes in a network, including those linked by both formal and informal connections. Formal connections represent official or prescribed relationships that are established based on the organizational structure, roles, and reporting lines. These connections are typically defined by job titles, positions, or hierarchical relationships within the organization. They reflect the formal communication channels and lines of authority through which work-related information, tasks, and decisions flow. Examples of formal connections include supervisor–subordinate relationships, team structures, and crossfunctional collaboration mandated by organizational policies. Informal connections, on the other hand, are unofficial relationships that develop naturally among employees in the organizations based on personal interactions, shared interests, or common goals. These connections are not prescribed by the formal organizational structure but emerge organically through social interactions and personal relationships. Informal connections can often transcend hierarchical boundaries and can exist across departments, teams, or even geographic locations. They are characterized by trust, shared experiences, shared values, mutual support, and collaboration that may not be reflected in formal relationships.

While formal connections are typically visible and documented within the organization chart, informal connections are more subtle and can be harder to capture through traditional organizational hierarchies. However, they play a significant role in shaping communication patterns, knowledge sharing, decision making, and overall organizational culture.

ONA seeks to understand (and visualize) both formal and informal connections within an organization. By mapping and analyzing these connections, organizations can gain insights into communication flows, collaboration patterns, information sharing, dynamics, and the overall social capital within an organization. This understanding can help identify influential individuals, communication bottlenecks, information gaps, and opportunities for fostering collaboration and innovation across formal and informal networks. Figure 5.5 illustrates how an influential individual or communication bottleneck could be identified.

Network size is an important factor to consider in ONA, because it can provide insights into the reach, influence, and diversity of an individual's connections within an organization. The size of an individual's network can indicate their potential access to diverse sources of information and knowledge. Those with larger networks have a broader reach and are more likely to receive timely and diverse information. Larger networks may be more complex and difficult to manage than smaller networks. Large networks may also have more diverse perspectives and ideas but may also suffer from more communication barriers and coordination challenges.

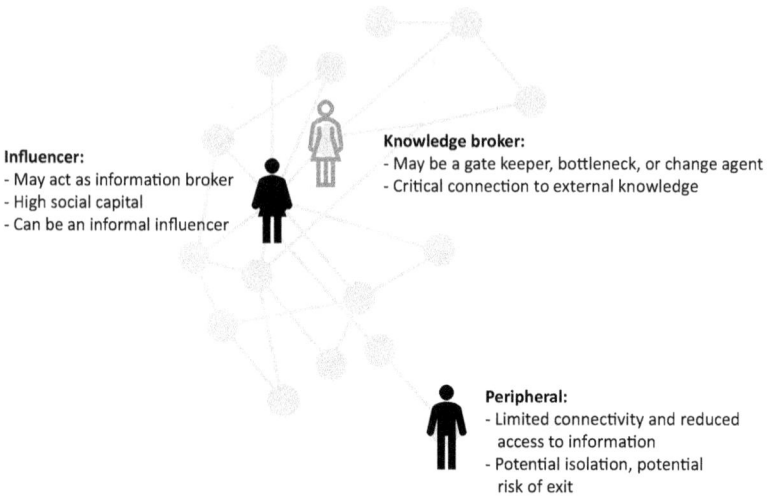

Influencer:
- May act as information broker
- High social capital
- Can be an informal influencer

Knowledge broker:
- May be a gate keeper, bottleneck, or change agent
- Critical connection to external knowledge

Peripheral:
- Limited connectivity and reduced access to information
- Potential isolation, potential risk of exit

Figure 5.5 Illustrative example of a network analysis

In addition to the overall network size, other measures can be used to describe the size and structure of different subgroups or clusters within a network. For example, measures such as group size and density can be used to identify clusters of individuals who are highly connected to each other. By analyzing network size and other related measures, ONA can provide insights into the overall structure and dynamics of organizational networks and help organizations identify ways to improve communication, collaboration, and innovation within and across different parts of their networks. It is important to note that network size alone does not guarantee effectiveness or success. The quality, strength, and diversity of connections also play a crucial role.

Network size could also play a role in the design and structure of a company. When designing the organizational structure, considering the network size of individuals can inform decisions about roles, responsibilities, and reporting lines. It can help determine the appropriate span of control for managers, the distribution of decision-making authority, and the allocation of resources. A consideration of network size can facilitate the formation of teams and collaboration structures that enhance communication, knowledge sharing, and innovation within the organization. Moreover, network size is connected to concepts such as social capital and the spread of information and influence within the company. By considering network size in the design of a company, organizations can strive to create an environment that promotes collaboration, reduces communication bottlenecks, and fosters effective decision-making processes.

Reach Index

When working at LinkedIn, my customers often looked at how they could increase their brand or spread information fast externally. Oftentimes, customers referred to the "six degrees of separation theory."[7] This theory suggests that any two people in the world can be connected through a chain of acquaintances with no more than six intermediaries. The theory emphasizes interconnectedness and the potential reach of social networks, such as LinkedIn. The reach index measures the degree of connectivity and accessibility of individuals within the organizational network. While the six degrees of separation theory and the reach index of ONA both deal with connectivity and relationships, they approach the concept from different perspectives.

The reach index is based on the concept of "reachability," which is the idea that some individuals are more reachable than others, because they have more direct or indirect connections to others within their network.

To calculate the reach index, first the set of people who are directly connected to a given individual in a network needs to be identified. It is followed by the set of people who are directly or indirectly connected to that individual through any number of intermediate connections. The reach index is calculated as the proportion of people in the overall network who can be reached through this set of direct and indirect connections.

Individuals with high reach indexes are seen as being well connected within their network with the potential to spread information quickly and efficiently. They are often referred to as brokers or connectors within the network and can play an important role in facilitating communication, collaboration, and innovation. Figure 5.5 illustrates a knowledge broker in the network. It also shows someone in the peripheral; this individual has a low reachability and potentially reduced access to information.

Bridging Index

Bridging index is a measure used in ONA to identify individuals who bridge different groups or subgroups within a network. In other words, the bridging index identifies people who connect otherwise disconnected parts of a network.

The bridging index is calculated by measuring the extent to which an individual has connections to people in different groups or clusters within their network. Specifically, it looks at the number of connections an individual has to people who are not part of their own immediate group or cluster and the degree to which those connections span different clusters or groups. Individuals with high bridging indexes are considered to be bridges between different groups and are often seen as key players in their network who can facilitate communication and collaboration between different parts of the organization.

By identifying individuals with high bridging indexes, ONA can help organizations understand the patterns of communications and collaboration within their networks and identify ways to improve communication and collaboration between different groups.

Influence Index

The influence index is a measure used in ONA to identify individuals who have the most influence or power within a network. The influence index is based on the idea that some individuals are more influential than others because they have more direct or indirect connections to others within their network.

This measure reflects the idea that individuals who are connected to other influential people are more likely to be influential themselves. Individuals with high influence indexes are often referred to as central actors within their networks and may have significant power to shape the flow of information and ideas within their networks. They may also be seen as key opinion leaders or decision makers within their organizations.

By identifying individuals with high influence indexes, ONA can help organizations understand the sources of power and influence within their networks and identify ways to leverage these individuals to improve communication, collaboration, and innovation.

Implementing and communicating new ideas within an organization are often carried out through a formal hierarchy, where leaders inform managers and managers, in turn, inform their teams. The aforementioned indexes could give a different perspective on how this process can be done more effectively. ONA can help identify who are the nonhierarchical influencers within an organization, and adoption and change can be achieved faster when leveraging the power and connections of these influencers. ONA can also be used to understand how decisions are being made within an organization, including who is involved, what factors influence the decisions, and how the decisions are being communicated.

Case: How Analysis Drives Changed Behavior in Meetings at VodafoneZiggo

At VodafoneZiggo,* I spoke with Joris van Hulzen, who leads the multidisciplinary people analytics and organizational development team, which was built four years ago. Overall, various skills are present within the core team, but there is also close collaboration with the rest of the organization, for example, with the central data science team. In recent years, team has made data-driven work as part of HR the norm. HR business partners and HR teams now use dashboards to access their insights to drive the business.

The team likes to start small, test hypotheses and experiment in order to disprove or substantiate hypotheses as quickly as possible. Sometimes, findings emerge that are not significant or have a smaller impact on the business; the findings then are shared and the related experiment is paused. Many organizations and teams find it difficult to pause analyses or projects that have already started, but I think that an advantage of experimenting is that when you decide not to carry on with one experiment, you have more time for others.

(Continues)

---

* VodafoneZiggo is a joint venture between Vodafone plc and Ziggo b.v. and is part of the Vodafone and Liberty Global group. It serves over 3.7 million households and 5.4 million mobile service customers and employs over 6,900 people. More at www.vodafoneziggo.nl/en/about-us/.

(*Continued*)

Within the organizational design part of the department, they use passive ONA to gain insights into how departments work together. For example, the team tries to answer questions such as: Are there departments that work together a lot or are there departments that do not collaborate often but should? These network analyses provide insights into patterns at the organizational level; they cannot be traced back to individuals to ensure privacy compliancy. The complexity of networks and collaboration patterns are analyzed, and these insights can indicate whether, for example, departments are in the right place, which then feeds the organizational design.

The team also uses ONA data to promote behavioral changes within the organization to improve collaboration. The team proactively shares information with the business units and their management about how the units are working together so that they can intervene at a unit or team level. This provides departments and teams with insights as a discussion starter about whether or not the collaboration behavior is desirable. An example of this is multitasking, which everyone within the organization knows is happening. When the data also confirms its existence and makes it transparent for department heads and managers, it is easier to address and discuss whether or not it is a desirable behavior. As such, more pointed questions then can be asked, such as: Are there too many people in meetings? Are meetings taking too long? Why do people multitask? Are there alternative ways for meeting that could help change this behavior?

Two results that Joris sees are that (1) on a qualitative level, he receives feedback from employees who indicate that it is nice that matters such as multitasking are discussed and that doing so gives a positive feeling to the team; and (2) on a quantitative level, he sees that meeting behavior is changing. The first aspect of behavior on a quantitative level that has changed is that the level of multitasking in meetings has gone down. In the initial analysis, employees multitasked during 37 percent of all meetings, and the majority of the meetings where employees multitasked had more than eight attendees. The behavior changed over time, and meetings with more than eight attendees reduced by 10.3 percent, and multitasking hours reduced by 21.5 percent. The other change that VodafoneZiggo has introduced is the concept of meeting guidelines, which prescribe general rules and tips for effective meetings. As part of these meeting guidelines, the importance of the so-called bumper time is stressed. This is time reserved between appointments. When an employee makes an appointment in Outlook for half an hour, the system automatically adjusts the length to 20 minutes and for an appointment of one hour to 45 minutes. These 10 or 15 minutes that employees then have between appointments can be used, for example, to work out their notes, send a presentation, get a cup of coffee, or walk to the next meeting room.

ONA for Hybrid Work

During and after the COVID-19 pandemic, relatively more of my customers were and have been looking into ways that ONA could help them plan for hybrid work. One way that ONA helps is by providing a clear understanding of how work is currently being done within an organization, which can help to identify potential bottlenecks or inefficiencies that may need to be addressed in order to effectively transition to a hybrid work model. For example, ONA can help to identify teams or individuals who are heavily reliant on in-person communication and collaboration and who may need additional support to adapt to a hybrid work environment.

ONA can also be used to identify the best way to structure teams and workflows in a hybrid work environment. By analyzing the current communication patterns within an organization, it is possible to identify which teams or individuals are most closely connected and rely on each other for support and which teams or individuals may be more isolated. This can help to inform decisions about which teams or individuals should be colocated and which can effectively work remotely. Overall, ONA can provide valuable insights into the way work is currently being done within an organization and can help to inform decisions about how to effectively transition to a hybrid work model. It can also help to identify potential challenges and opportunities and can be used to develop strategies and plans to ensure a smooth and successful transition.

It is important to note that ONA, like any other method, has its limitations, such as availability and accuracy of data. Some organizations may have a culture of not being open to sharing information, so collecting data may be difficult. Additionally, it is important to have the right tools, such as network graphs and expertise, as described later, to effectively analyze the data and interpret the results.

Skills Needed in People Analytics

A people analytics department typically requires a combination of technical and business skills. Some of the critical skills needed are described next.

- *Data analytics skills*: People analytics involves working with large amounts of data, so proficiency in data analysis is a must. This includes understanding statistical analysis, data visualization, and predictive modeling.
- *Technology skills*: People analytics departments require individuals who are comfortable working with technology, including database management and data warehousing.
- *Data science skills*: In a people analytics department, data science skills are highly relevant for individuals, as their work involves working with large sets of data to derive insights and solve business problems. Where analytical skills can be sufficient for reporting, for more sophisticated analyses, data scientist skills such as programming and ML are required.
- *Business acumen skills*: People analytics professionals should be able to understand companies' goals and how data could support reaching those goals. This involves having a strong understanding of the business strategy and key performance indicators (KPIs).
- *Communication skills*: People analytics professionals need to be able to communicate their findings effectively to a variety of audiences, including executives, managers, and employees. This requires strong verbal and written communication skills.
- *Data visualization and storytelling skills*: It is important in a people analytics department to be able to communicate analysis findings in a compelling and impactful way. Visual

techniques help to communicate insights more effectively by having the right narrative for the right audience. Sometimes, a message delivered to an executive team is different and focused on business outcomes, whereas a message to employees might focus on the benefits of an improved individual employee experience.

- *Critical thinking skills*: The ability to analyze data and identify patterns requires critical thinking skills. People analytics professionals should be able to ask the right questions, challenge assumptions, and make data-driven decisions even if doing so goes against everyone's instincts. The ability to spot when data is missing, wrong, misleading or misrepresented is also a crucial skill.

- *Collaboration skills*: People analytics departments often work closely with other departments, such as HR and IT, so the ability to collaborate effectively is essential.

- *Ethical skills*: People analytics departments work with sensitive employee data, so professionals in this field should have a strong understanding of ethical considerations and data privacy laws. They should be committed to protecting employee privacy and ensuring that data is used responsibly.

Case: How LinkedIn Measures Culture Through People Analytics

One of my favorite examples of people analytics in practice comes from a story told to me by David White, VP of People Analytics at LinkedIn.[†] Culture has always been important for both David and LinkedIn, which I experienced firsthand when I was employed at the company. In 2017, David worked with Christina Hall, LinkedIn's then chief human resources officer (CHRO), and they measured

---

(Continues)

[†] Founded in 2003, LinkedIn connects the world's professionals to make them more productive and successful. With more than 850 million members worldwide, including executives from every Fortune 500 company, LinkedIn is the world's largest professional network. The company has around 25,000 employees. More information at www.linkedin.com/company/linkedin/about/.

(Continued)

culture. Culture can be a very difficult parameter to measure. It is not quantitative but rather qualitative—it is how employees perceive the company's culture. Culture can change based on whom organizations hire. If leaders or middle managers who do not align with an organization's current culture are hired, the organization can be in trouble, because, over time, the culture may change in a way that is unfavorable to the organization. Culture is only equal to behaviors. It is a system of values and beliefs that shapes how work gets done. Culture is how we interact to get tasks done within a company. Culture only matters if it helps the business achieve business results. That is why culture across industries can be significantly different; in the manufacturing industry, for example, a safety culture can be much more important than a caring culture, which might be more important in the tech industry.

When David and his team started to conduct the culture analysis at LinkedIn, one of the insights that this study revealed was that culture is inextricably tied to the executive team, primarily the CEO. Culture does not happen from the bottom up. The study was conducted at the end of 2017 and the beginning of 2018, when LinkedIn was under CEO Jeff Weiner's iconic leadership. At this time, the shared values, beliefs, and practices associated with these values were deeply and consistently ingrained throughout the entire organization, resulting in a strong culture.

In order to understand the organizational culture, the people analytics team analyzed all the transcribed data from the company's all hands.[‡] The analysis started with a basic word analysis of all hands'

[‡] An all-hands meeting is a gathering of all employees. The purpose of the meeting is to provide updates, share important news, and discuss relevant topics. All-hands meetings typically involve the entire company, from senior executives to entry-level employees and are usually held on a regular basis, in LinkedIn's case, biweekly. During the meeting, the CEO and/or other top leaders present company performance metrics, goals for the upcoming quarter, and updates on major initiatives and projects. It is an important way for leaders to communicate with the organization and to promote transparency, foster communication and collaboration, and ensure all employees are informed and engaged.

transcripts to inform the team of the points that the executive leadership team was sharing and what they were emphasizing during the meetings. The transcription showed that the most frequently mentioned value was results.

Behaviors are closely associated with values because values are the beliefs or principles that people use to guide their behaviors. Values shape how people perceive the world around them and what they consider important, which in turn affect the choices that they make and the actions that they take. For example, if someone values honesty, they are likely to be truthful in their behavior and avoid lying or being deceitful. Values can serve as a moral compass that guides behavior. When employees act in accordance with their organization's values, they often experience a sense of fulfillment and purpose. Conversely, when their behavior conflicts with their organization's values, they may experience feelings of guilt or dissatisfaction. LinkedIn has 11 values, and it might be logical to look at the behaviors associated with these values when conducting an analysis. However, David and his team decided otherwise. Instead of conducting a survey with potentially more than 70 associated behaviors, they created a survey with only 12 items. For each of the 11 values, the survey asked respondents to indicate the degree to which they saw the value demonstrated at work by choosing responses from a five-point Likert scale. There was also an optional field where employees could share how they saw the value demonstrated at work. At the end, there was one question where employees were asked to indicate what other behaviors they thought were part of the LinkedIn culture but are not named in its 11 values.

The survey's outcome showed what employees saw as the most important values. It also showed what words were most associated with each value; with each value, employees could list the words that they thought of when considering the value. For example, employees associated the value "relationships matter" with the words "friend" and "lunch." Understanding the words associated with each value is important because people can interpret values differently. For an

(*Continues*)

(*Continued*)

organization, it is important that the perception of employees is in line with the expectations of its leadership in order to make sure that culture contributes to achieving business results.

The key is that culture is inextricably tied to leadership. Thus, David and his team took the executive team's survey results and compared them to the employees' results. If the executive team knows what the culture should be in order to achieve their business results, but the employees have a different idea of what the culture is, then a gap exists that is important to understand. Moreover, if there is a gap, it is important to understand how to close it.

For example, if "relationships matter" means something else for the executive team than it does for employees, then there needs to be a change in the behaviors shared and shown by the executive team in order to bridge that gap. Another example is the value "taking intelligent risks." This is a very important value for the business, but it was ranked the lowest by the employees, while the employees ranked the value "relationships matter" the highest. These are conflicting values, and relationships should be an enabler when taking intelligent risks, not a value that slows it down if employees feel that taking risks could harm their relationships. After the analysis, the CEO and his executive team tried to maintain the culture and bridge the gap between what the executive team expected and what the employees demonstrated as behaviors. So, one of the actions that the executive team took was that they presented about taking intelligent risks during an all hands, and they defined the behavioral expectations associated with taking intelligent risks. This helped employees understand what the expected behaviors are from the leadership and how those are connected to each value of the organization.

After the 2018 analysis, one follow-up analysis was done to measure if the intentional communication strategy contributed to the intended change. In 2023, the next analysis is being planned, and it will be interesting, as it is a cultural analysis being conducted after the COVID-19 pandemic and a CEO change. This survey could demonstrate different behaviors and a different ranking of how the values are demonstrated than the previous one. The behaviors of every individual changed so much and will continue to change in this ever-changing world of work. These insights will be extremely valuable, and I applaud LinkedIn for continuing to do this. I would encourage other organizations to start measuring their values and how culture contributes to their business needs.

Conclusion

People analytics has emerged as a powerful tool for organizations to leverage data to improve their human capital management. By analyzing data on employee behavior, performance, and other relevant metrics, organizations can gain valuable insights into how to optimize their workforce and drive better business outcomes. It is important to recognize that people analytics is not a linear process. It requires a continuous cycle of data collection, analysis, and experimentation with ongoing refinement and iteration based on the results.

ONA is a valuable tool for understanding the relationships, communication patterns, and information flow within an organization. It goes beyond traditional hierarchies and focuses on informal connections and interactions. ONA helps identify influential individuals, uncover hidden dynamics, and evaluate collaboration efficiency. It enables organizations to foster knowledge sharing, innovation, and crossfunctional collaboration. ONA supports diversity and inclusion initiatives by identifying patterns of exclusion or underutilization. However, ONA should be complemented with qualitative analysis, feedback mechanisms, and an understanding of organizational culture. Implementing ONA requires transparency, trust, and action. Overall, ONA provides insights to optimize networks, foster innovation, and create an agile work environment in an interconnected world.

As organizations increasingly rely on people analytics, it is essential to prioritize the protection of employee privacy. While the use of data can provide valuable insights, it is important to ensure that employee privacy is respected and that data is collected and used in a responsible and ethical manner.

CHAPTER 6

Metaverse

Over the past few years, my customers' interest in the metaverse has sharply grown, reflected in the increasing number of conversations that I have had with them on the subject. When I started to write this book about the impact of technology on employee experience, the metaverse needed to be addressed, and more background information needed to be disseminated. I noticed that my customers sometimes feared missing out. The overall interest in the metaverse has grown over the last few years, and Facebook's and other large organizations' increased investment in mixed reality and the metaverse has accelerated the trend. Mixed reality has been around for a while but has not yet entered the field of HR at large (nor has the metaverse). Although it is still in development, the metaverse could totally change the way we work and add value to our employee experience. Organizations are currently focused on determining when it will actually be part of our daily lives and how it will look, and along the way, large investments are being made. Gartner predicts that by 2026, 25 percent of people will spend at least one hour a day in the metaverse for work, shopping, education, social interaction, and/or entertainment and 30 percent of organizations will have products and services ready for the metaverse.[1] Organizations are putting metaverse strategies in place for their overall *business* goals; however, there are not that many organizations that have created a strategy on how the metaverse contributes to reaching their *people* goals. While the metaverse is an interesting new technology and organizations might fear missing out if they do not embrace it, I want to stress the importance of assessing the metaverse's actual value to the business and people strategies of organizations before they implement it.

One thing that many organizations have learned is that having a clear strategy is important when implementing new technologies. Before the COVID-19 pandemic, many organizations were not ready and did not have a clear strategy in place for hybrid work. The changing circumstances forced organizations to experiment and learn fast and discover what pros and cons are for their organization and its workforce. These experimentations allowed organizations to adjust policies and pivot more agile strategies. Hybrid work became indispensable for many organizations, where prior to the pandemic, discussions on implementing hybrid work generated more resistance. With the world of work changing fast, acting without a clear strategy is costly, especially if external factors demand organizations to pivot their strategy quickly without room for experimentation or learning. Therefore, even if organizations are not entering the metaverse today, it is worthwhile to think about the long-term strategy and if and how to experiment and implement it in the future.

What Is the Metaverse?

There is no consensus yet on what the metaverse is or whom it is for. The metaverse is a digital space virtually inhabited by people, places, things, and processes. Gartner refers to it as the next iteration of the Internet that started as individual bulletin boards and independent online destinations. Eventually, these destinations became sites on a virtual shared space; this is similar to how the metaverse will continue to develop. Often it is misrepresented as VR, where VR is merely a way to experience the metaverse. The metaverse is also like the Internet in that it is neither device dependent nor owned by a single organization.

Before I explain how the metaverse is currently defined, I want to share a brief overview of the evolution of the metaverse and its terms. The term metaverse was coined in Neal Stephenson 's 1992 science fiction novel *Snow Crash*, in which humans, as programmable avatars, interact with each other and software agents, in a 3D virtual space that is a metaphor of the real world. In the novel, Stephenson uses the term "metaverse" to describe a VR-based successor to the Internet.[2] The metaverse is a complex and evolving concept and its formation involves several key components. The development generally relies on the convergence of various technologies and interconnected systems, such as digital twins.

In 2002, Michael Grieves introduced the concept and model of the digital twin during a presentation at the University of Michigan.

The premise driving the model is that each system consists of two systems: a physical system that has always existed and a new virtual system that contains all of the information about the physical system.[3] Accordingly, there is a mirroring or twinning of systems between what exists in real space and what exists in virtual space. Simply put, a digital twin is the digital counterpart of a physical object. A digital twin is not specifically a metaverse construct. While both concepts involve virtual representations, they have different purposes and scopes. While digital twins can be part of the data and infrastructure that support the metaverse, they are not inherently the same thing. Digital twins are focused on representing and optimizing specific objects or systems, whereas the metaverse is a larger-scale virtual world that can contain numerous digital twins and other virtual constructs.

Some people refer to the metaverse as the next version of Second Life, which is a 3D virtual world created in 2003 by Linden Lab. Second Life is an early example of a metaverse, where users create their own avatars and interact with each other in a fully immersive 3D environment. When I try to explain the metaverse to my kids and offer them a framework, I refer to Roblox, launched in 2006, which is super popular with younger generations. Roblox offers 3D virtual spaces in a virtual universe. By providing tools and a platform, it empowers people to create their own immersive experience by leveraging these tools. Roblox is also building a virtual economy powered by a community of creators and users, and they claim that any creator can make a living across digital and physical goods and services. The gaming industry continued to evolve and build toward better immersive experiences, with the introductions of the once very popular Pokémon Go, a game that uses AR technology to overlay a virtual world onto the real world, and later Fortnite. Fortnite is a popular online video game, where a large number of players compete against each other in a virtual arena. Fortnite has been recognized as one of the early examples of a metaverse-like experience. The events organized in Fortnite attracted massive audiences, blurring the lines between virtual entertainment and real-world experiences. It has played a role in popularizing and promoting the concept of the metaverse in the mainstream consciousness.

Now, it is also evolving to the business world for multiple purposes, with the announcement of Mesh* by Microsoft and Meta investing more heavily in the metaverse. Fully immersive experiences are a big step from the current digital experiences employees and consumers experience. Growth rates vary and investors expressed some concerns, resulting in partially shifting priorities. Alignment with investors and stakeholders is needed and the rate of adoption and scale of the metaverse depends on it.

The metaverse will probably not replace the Internet but is more of an iteration and is built upon the Internet to iteratively transform it. Instead of visiting the Internet and its webpages, we will enter the Internet or will be "within" it. To form a complete metaverse, multiple technologies need to be combined, such as digital twins, the digitization of real-world objects, and 3D-streaming technology. The technologies exist, but they require improved computing power, and the needed hardware is currently too expensive to reach the masses. This can slow down the scale at which the metaverse will be used. Although not necessary, VR headsets are being promoted and used for entering the metaverse; however, consumer VR headsets still cost around 400 dollars (and up to 3,000 dollars). Some people also start to feel dizzy or get nauseas when wearing a headset, and it makes them experience motion sickness; this is expected to improve as the technology matures. Another factor slowing down the progress is network availability; not everywhere in the world is there the same quality of bandwidth and Internet reliability. Cyberattacks, such as invisibly eavesdropping and manipulating users into actual physical harm, are also raised by researchers as possible threats to the metaverse.[4] Moreover, as of yet, there is no interoperability, which is the ability to take an individual's data with them when they go from place to place (e.g., their own avatar with them when they enter a different world). Currently, it is decentralized and Meta, Microsoft, Epic, and others own people's data when they enter their worlds, but smaller places exist where people can own their own data. Lastly, as a society, we have

---

* Microsoft Mesh is a platform designed for virtual collaboration across different platforms. It enables shared experiences from anywhere and on any device through mixed-reality applications. More at www.microsoft.com/mesh.

not figured out what policies, protocols, and operating standards will exist for the metaverse, and this is a huge challenge. Having an open protocol is probably needed to reach scale.

What Opportunities Does the Metaverse Offer to Employees?

Within the full employee life cycle, there are opportunities for the metaverse to start playing a role. The Microsoft Work Trend Index 2022 states that 52 percent of employees are open to using digital immersive spaces in the metaverse for meetings or team activities in the next year. "Avatars and the metaverse bring us one step closer to making people feel like they're together even when they are physically apart," says Maria Gonzalez Franco, principal researcher at Microsoft Research. "Our early research shows that when compared to an audio-only call, people feel more engaged, more present, and even more comfortable when using an avatar in a meeting."[5] The metaverse can go from being an experiential space to transforming the traditional employee experience. Within this new hybrid or even remote world, virtual tools and avatars could help create more bespoke experiences and improve the employee experience through the entire employee life cycle.

Key Scenarios and Initial Use Cases

The HR industry is not always a front runner when it comes to implementing new technologies and innovating, as doing so can be a big investment and too experimental. As the metaverse redesigns the way we work, there could be major implications for HR leaders. HR teams might drive this transformation. Not only does HR have the necessary know-how needed to implement these changes, but they also have the responsibility to design the future of work with people in mind. To effectively drive this transformation to the metaverse, HR may need to acquire certain tools and knowledge. HR teams should have a solid understanding of the technologies underpinning the metaverse, such as VR, AR, and other related hardware and software, and collaborate closely with their IT counterparts in gaining this technology proficiency. They should familiarize themselves with virtual collaboration platforms, digital communication tools, and VR training solutions. Staying up to date on emerging technologies and trends is crucial. The metaverse also generates vast amounts of data, which can be leveraged for various HR and workforce purposes, including talent acquisition, performance management, and employee experience. HR teams should develop data analytics skills to learn how to extract meaningful insights from metaverse-related data. HR also needs to adopt recruitment strategies for the metaverse era.

The metaverse presents legal and ethical challenges that HR must address. Understanding the legal implications of virtual workplaces, data protection regulations, intellectual property rights, and ethical considerations is essential. Collaboration with legal and compliance teams is therefore crucial. I believe that there is potential for such innovation to be applied throughout the candidate and employee experiences, and I want to share these possibilities. Some organizations are already experimenting, and I have included some examples even if the outcomes of the investments are not known yet, because doing so brings the possibilities to life.

Brand and Recruit

When I started at LinkedIn in 2012, many of my customers were still focused on traditional ways of recruiting. Over the past decade, leveraging more (matching) technology and data has become the norm in the world of recruitment. The metaverse could open new avenues to engage and bring organizations and their recruiters and candidates closer together, starting at the beginning of the candidate experience.

Employer Branding

As brands are increasingly expected to act as platforms that broadcast their ideas and values, there is a big potential for virtual worlds. With the in-game advertising market size expected to grow by 10.97 billion dollars by 2024, signs point to gaming as the future for advertising.[6] In my view, there is an opportunity for employer branding in the metaverse. Organizations are starting to look more at skills, which are required for or shown in certain games. This creates room for employers to demonstrate to people who have the related skills how they could use them if hired. This could bring new possibilities to the world of employer branding. The metaverse could also change standard and sometimes dull job descriptions and bring jobs more to life. It could provide a virtual sense to candidates, so that they can experience a job before applying. For example, a virtual world could already give a virtual representation of a physical plant, store, hospital, factory, or office in which the candidate would work and a representation of the stakeholders with whom the candidate would deal. Where LinkedIn reformed the job market, the metaverse could revolutionize the candidate experience, starting with a virtual job market. Samsung has already held a recruitment fair that allowed candidate participation from anywhere at any time through a platform called Gather.[7] It allowed participants to take a virtual tour of the company's facilities, including entire sites and plants. The participants were also provided with extensive information about the company, its job openings, and its corporate culture. To encourage more engagement, real-time chatting was possible with both recruiters and representatives from the business.

Recruiting

Currently, recruiters still spend part of their time hunting and screening candidates. The metaverse has the potential to allow recruiters to conduct more meaningful observations and assessments throughout a candidate's journey. The metaverse could offer talent communities that are safe spaces for candidates and that allow candidates to have more one-on-one interactions, while also having access to more information about organizations with job vacancies before they choose to apply. The same applies for recruiters; they can have one-on-one interactions that are warmer than traditional outreach techniques, such as through a job board or LinkedIn, and can more easily "convince" candidates to apply. PwC created Virtual Park, a metaverse platform for hosting recruitment fairs. PwC sees the platform as an opportunity to attract a wider range of individuals, which is important from a diversity and inclusion standpoint. Within the first six months, Virtual Park hosted over 12,400 unique users across 56 recruitment events.[8]

Interviews and Assessment

We all have had the classic interview question: "what you would do if a customer started doing something?" where "something" refers to anything that happens within your line of work. For example, a shift leader candidate might be asked: "What would you do if an employee pulls you into a conversation with an unhappy customer who is becoming aggressive?" Traditional interview techniques allow interviewers to dig deep but are still hypothetical or based on past behavior. The metaverse will allow organizations to recreate a virtual representation of a described scenario and assess the actual skills needed to handle the situation. Such an approach will make it easier to not only assess if a candidate is the right hire but also give immediate input for a candidate's learning and development plan once hired.

Onboarding

Well before the COVID-19 pandemic, a *Forbes* article stated that 28 percent of employees left their jobs within the first 90 days[9] due to poor onboarding, and a Gallup report found that only 12 percent of employees reflected favorably on job onboarding experiences.[10] Employees who onboarded over the past two years were in need of extra support. The Microsoft Work Trend Index shows that employees hired since March 2020, due to remote onboarding, which reached its greatest prevalence during the COVID-19 pandemic, are less likely to feel included, have weaker relationships with their teams, and are at greater risk of attrition than employees that were hired prepandemic.[11]

The metaverse engages new employees and creates new immersive onboarding experiences through persistent spaces. It can provide an immersive experience for newcomers to enter the virtual world of their new employers by visualizing the organizational structure and the physical office building. These virtual tours around a company can be of the campus or offices, but they could also be of factories and plants to create a better understanding of how the company operates for information workers without requiring them to actually visit the physical plant or factory. The metaverse provides interaction and meeting with colleagues throughout different departments and geographies and through all layers of the organization. Being welcomed by a CEO in the metaverse can add more of a personal touch than a prerecorded video. The metaverse also offers gamified learning experiences for onboarding and training. For example, organizations could offer a scavenger hunt to familiarize candidates with a building instead of a standard tour. As an onboarding solution in the metaverse, Accenture created a virtual campus called One Accenture Park, with which it introduces new hires to the company. In the metaverse, employees arrive at Accenture's Nth Floor, where they meet, learn, and collaborate in new ways.[12] For frontline workers, Toyota Material Handling has introduced VR to onboard service technicians with the company's complex inventory in a collaborative, multiplayer setting by using VR vision for the creation of content on a 3D platform, as well as learning management system integration and a Meta Quest headset to create VR training programs. This grants all staff members access to all machines, regardless of the machine's or employee's location, which is impossible in real life.[13]

Case: Saving Costs by Training New Hires in the Metaverse

At a large Fortune 500 company that manufacturers tires, new hires need to be trained. The metaverse offers instructors, mentors, and managers the ability to participate in training or the supervising of an employee regardless of their location. Historically, the company has conducted training by taking the most senior employee on the factory floor and pairing them together with the recently hired junior employee. Together they stand in the factory by a tire assembly machine, and they build tires together. The senior employee teaches the junior employee how to do the job. With this teaching method, there are many challenges. One is that the tire assembly

(Continues)

(*Continued*)

machine has to be taken offline. As a result, it is not producing tires, which is how the company makes its revenue, and it generates an incredible amount of waste. Over 28,000 tires a year are wasted just in raw material from training on such a machine. The other issue is that this training method takes the most experienced workers out of production. They are not building the tires, but rather they are spending their time training an employee. Overall, addressing all of these business drivers is a compelling reason to find an alternative way to do this training. What Altoura[†] offers and allows this Fortune 500 company to do is to digitize or create a digital twin or digital cousin.[‡] The manufacturer uses a virtual 3D model of the piece of equipment that has all of the necessary parts with which trainees need to interact. Pieces that do not have any relevance to what they are trying to do are not uploaded to the 3D model. This 3D model simulates what it is like to build actual tires. The business value of this approach is that new employees can be trained anywhere in the world. They do not have to be on the factory floor. They can be in a classroom or they can even be at home. Another added value is that the tire assembly machine can be in production 24 hours a day, building products instead of being used for training, allowing for a reduction in wasted raw material, from 28,000 wasted tires down to about 1,700. The company can also go from one-on-one training to one to many; one instructor can train 10 employees at a time, because they can all be networked together in the 3D model.

Another example is a global company that has used the Altoura technology to train technicians on different processes for maintaining

---

[†] Altoura is the pioneer of interactive digital twin technology and the maker of a productivity platform for spatial work. Altoura's no-code platform imports and transforms 3D assets into immersive, interactive, and collaborative spatial workflows, such as immersive training and design visualization. More at www .altoura.com.
[‡] A digital twin is a virtual representation of the real world, including physical objects, processes, relationships, and behaviors. Jamie Fleming prefers to use the term "digital cousin" instead of "digital twin."

engines. What this company found is that it can cut the duration of its traditional training process in half. The hours that technicians can actually be servicing engines instead of training equate to millions of dollars of just billable time.

The return on investment further emphasizes that there is a compelling business reason to shift different business processes into the metaverse to allow people to collaborate interactively and to do simulations.

Learn and Develop

The easier and more convenient employers make learning for their employees, the better. The metaverse combines reality and VR, and this blending of both worlds makes it possible to create unique training opportunities. Employees would not just be looking at informative presentations or learning theories; they would be practicing as well. From surgeons to fighter pilots, from learning to cope with customer aggression and robberies in retail, to operating highly technical machinery, the practical approach that the metaverse offers could be a perfect simulation solution, allowing employees to train precisely, realistically, and fast. Simulations have already been part of a few industries, such as medical and pilot training, but the metaverse could bring it to other learning environments as well.

The metaverse could allow organizations to simulate real problems with concrete solutions and see the results. If their results are not good enough or mistakes are identified, employees can simply try again until they succeed, without the fear of doing something actually wrong that could cause danger in the physical world. Soft skills are very important when it comes to being successful in the workplace, especially when dealing with customers. Organizations can create multiple scenarios that are experienced often and play through them as many times as they like until a satisfied outcome is reached. Teams and individual performance reviews can be carried out using escape rooms in which a variety of skills are measured and analysis are created and reported. Future Workplace, an HR advisory firm, and Mursion, a VR training platform, found that 200 out of 300 learning and development (L&D) leaders surveyed reported that they had already implemented a VR training program for soft skills or planned to implement one within the next two years.[14]

To help employees improve their presentation skills, Cognizant developed a multistage, VR-driven training program. First, new hires complete an interactive digital course on data-driven storytelling. Next, they practice giving a client presentation with a VR avatar that plays the role of a customer. Finally, an AI analyzes the presentation for keywords, emotions, tones, and body language and turns that analysis into actionable feedback for the user. This capacity for immediate feedback and essentially limitless rounds of practice (without relying on expensive, human training resources) is a key advantage of VR-powered learning tools.[15]

The need to learn a new language is still common in the business world. Only studying vocabulary and conjugations is not the way to learn a language; it requires an immersive learning environment, and practicing in the real world and real conversations help employees learn languages the fastest.

New immersive learning experiences that improve the efficacy of virtual training for employees make learning fun, exciting, and engaging, while reducing travel and logistics costs. The case of the virtual store explained by Altoura's CEO Jamie Fleming in Chapter 1 is a perfect example that speaks to the reduction of travel costs by allowing employees to learn in the virtual instead of the physical world. The technology to enable organizations to design innovative and groundbreaking L&D processes is arriving and much more is to come. So, I would advise organizations to think through how their employees' experiences can be improved.

Case: Solving the 10-Million-Dollar Problem

Another customer of Altoura was spending over 10 million dollars a year on service calls for equipment that was not broken. The people who were operating this equipment were very junior employees, often with small skill sets and without much work experience. When the equipment was not performing as anticipated, their first reaction was to call a service technician and to stop the use of the equipment. What the company found was that there was nothing wrong with the equipment. There was just a lack of education on how to use the equipment. This was a 10-million-dollar problem that the company tried to solve by allowing its employees to use Altoura to help them quickly diagnose the problem.

Entering the metaverse forced the junior hires to go through a simulation of how to digitally troubleshoot the equipment. Only if they could not solve the problem through troubleshooting could they call the technician. By reducing the time in which the equipment was used and frequency with which technicians had to be called saved the company millions of dollars.

Engage and Retain

Employees have new expectations, and many organizations have seen decreases in their engagement scores. Well-being, mental health, flexible work options, and better connections are priorities. The metaverse brings people together with a sense of presence through immersive spaces even when individuals are physically apart. The majority of hybrid and remote employees feel lonelier at work than before they went hybrid or remote, and that has had a negative impact on their well-being and productivity and also led to an increase in the risk of burnout.[16] Compared to an audio-call, when using an avatar in a meeting, people feel more engaged, more present, and even more comfortable. With an avatar, employees do not have to worry how they look; it creates a lot of flexibility in how people want to present themselves. This means that employees can present the best digital and authentic versions of themselves at all times and within all parts of the organization. Employees can create their own avatars in tools like Ready Player Me, which makes it possible to use the same avatar across different platforms, so employees can bring their own virtual self to work. Organizations such as Microsoft and Meta are also investing in avatars, with Microsoft also introducing 3D representations to the Teams platform.

Virtual Collaboration

Virtual collaboration brings people together to interact and collaborate in natural ways, as if they are physically present in the same room. This might involve not only brainstorming and whiteboarding sessions but also immersive meetings, such as daily standups or product reviews. Meta with Horizon Workrooms,[§] Microsoft with Mesh,[**] and CoVince with The Gathering[††] are bringing the metaverse to work through virtual collaboration solutions. In place of starting a video call or sending a message to a colleague, these platforms allow employees to meet in the metaverse where they have avatars and a space to collaborate. Meeting in the metaverse is different from video calling in that employees feel like they are in a well-designed meeting room, and it allows employees to interact within the same environment, for example, by drawing on a whiteboard and even moving around objects in the virtual room. The virtual 3D versions of employees can nod and raise their hands as if they were in a physical space, making the experience more real than looking at their screen with multiple camera feeds with different backgrounds (or even worse, looking at black screens or profile pictures of colleagues who have turned off their cameras). The sound is also different; whereas with a conference or video call the sound comes from one direction, the metaverse makes use of spatial audio. This means that the sound appears to originate from the source. The first time I had a meeting in the metaverse, it was really surprising that it was possible to have side conversations, as the further away I moved from one conversation the quieter its audio became and the closer

---

[§] Workrooms is a virtual space that brings teams together in the metaverse. It helps employees to feel truly present with their co-workers and get more done with cutting-edge collaboration tools. More information at meta.com/work/workrooms.

[**] Microsoft Mesh enables presence and shared experiences from anywhere—on any device—through mixed-reality applications. More information at microsoft.com/en-us/mesh.

[††] The Gathering makes events, meetings, and collaboration more fun and effective. It brings teams together to train, present, and organize their workflows in personalized environments. More information at http://covince.com.

I moved to another small group of people the louder their conversation became. It was incredible to see that when a person on my right started talking, everybody also turned their heads to the right, as if we were in a physical meeting.

A metaverse event is an event held in a virtual environment rather than a physical one. So instead of going to a concert hall or a stadium, employees attend an event via a device from their home or any other location. Whereas a physical event would provide a limited number of places and require employees to travel, a virtual event has unlimited places and can be joined from anywhere. With their avatars, employees can move between different rooms, from the virtual coffee corner to the virtual pool, and interact with other employees and build connections across the globe informally, easily, and at scale. Virtual events provide a great opportunity for inclusion. Oftentimes, employees who are located in regions away from a company's headquarters cannot attend company meetings, such as town halls, and even local employees have obligations that prevent them from attending a physical event. Virtual events not only offer the possibility for every employee to attend more flexibly, but they also remove language barriers. With real-time translation, employees can speak to anyone from anywhere regardless of whether or not they are speaking the same language. Moreover, physical events can offer limited accessibility to employees who have limited physical mobility, whereas they can move around more easily in the metaverse. The same applies to employees who are deaf or hearing impaired. Using closed captions or sign language can allow employees to communicate with every other employee in the room.

Focusing on social hubs and software that allow colleagues to connect in a single virtual setting could prevent employees from feeling isolated. Virtual water cooler or coffee chats in the metaverse could help employees build strong connections throughout an organization regardless of their location. This could enable a better and faster information flow across regions and departments. Birthdays and Christmas parties can be celebrated more inclusively, allowing everyone to participate and connect. The metaverse can provide a fun and easy way for people to mingle, play games, and hang out in immersive spaces.

Case: Next-Level Hybrid Collaboration in a Collaboration Park

In Chapter 2, I wrote about the five stages for hybrid work and about how some organizations are strategizing toward more personalized hybrid work, while others are still replicating the work that employees used to do in the office but which they now do from home. When I spoke with Melanie van Halteren and Richard van Tilborg, the cofounders of CoVince,[‡‡] they showed me work that they have done with a few of their clients to create hybrid collaboration parks.

Hybrid collaboration parks are innovative e-workspaces designed to promote collaboration, innovation, and creativity among companies and their employees. These parks typically provide a variety of spaces, resources, and services that allow employees to collaborate and share ideas from any location and, in the case of CoVince, also from any device. In a hybrid collaboration park, there are typically traditional office spaces as well as shared spaces, such as meeting rooms, co-working spaces, and even event spaces. What sets hybrid collaboration parks apart is their focus on fostering a community of collaboration and innovation. To achieve this, they offer various programs and events. These activities are designed to bring together employees from different parts of an organization and encourage them to share ideas and work together on projects.

A collaboration park that Melanie and Richard showed me was for a city government, with which they created a virtual Obeya.[§§] This unique collaboration park combines all the advantages of physical and digital spaces into one central hub to support crossfunctional meetings and virtual collaboration. It moves away from the monotony that employees often experience in more traditional video conferencing and creates a more social experience. In the case of the

---

[‡‡] CoVince designed a metaverse platform that fosters learning, collaboration, and community. More at https://connect.covince.com/www/english/home.html.
[§§] Obeya means "big room" in Japanese, and it is often used to visually represent the tasks and goals of an organization. This creates an overview and fosters better and more effective collaboration.

Obeya, it helped the city government to have an overview of the entire governmental strategy and to see the connections between all of the programs that they had created while building the strategy, as illustrated in Figure 6.1. Before the Obeya, the employees had often not been aware of projects that existed in other parts of the organization, let alone of how all these projects were connected. The visual representation showed how everything was connected, and this led to better collaboration and more productivity, and some employees even found it more fun to collaborate in this way. The rooms allow for better collaboration, because employees can go from one virtual project room to another and see who is working there. The closer one employee moves to another employee, because of the use of spatial sound, the louder they become, similar to how in the physical world, when you walk up to a colleague, you can hear them typing or talking to another person on the phone. Employees also make use of their personal dashboards, which include a dynamic timeline that keeps employees up to date on their organization's news and announcements. The dashboards also include task management tools to help employees stay on top of their own to-do lists while also understanding the other tasks of the project. The Obeya encourages employees to go from one project room to another, and its setup fosters more spontaneous encounters.

Figure 6.1 Visual representation of the Obeya

(*Continues*)

(*Continued*)

The difficulty with implementing this new technology is getting employees to change their behaviors and adopt a new way of working. To make sure that employees stay in the collaboration park and are engaged, there are also AI-powered virtual assistants that can help employees with many tasks, such as brainstorming. For me, the beauty of these parks is that they give a very clear overview of everything that is going on in an organization, and when it is not visualized, it is sometimes hard for the human brain to understand how many projects employees work on at one time. One other visualization that Melanie and Richard showed me was that of a train with all of its carriages representing a different project. Every time a project is added, a new train carriage is created. As a leader, it is very hard to ignore the breadth of projects. If there are too many projects, a visualization such as this one can make it easier to create focus. Employees can also walk from one carriage to another and, in this way, can work on different projects throughout the day. In the carriage, there are data spaces that show all kinds of valuable insights related to the project and tasks related to various KPIs. The leader of this project has access to data space where all data from the various projects is visualized in real time. This can contribute to optimizing the business operations of any organization, improve project performance, and allow the organization to make more evidence-based decisions.

Offboard and Rehire

I have not yet seen an organization that uses the metaverse for offboarding or rehiring purposes. However, I do think that such an application could be possible in the future. As a LinkedIn alumna myself, I am part of its vast alumni network. LinkedIn has a platform where alumni can communicate, receive newsletters, and organize events. Similar to the branding and recruiting examples shown earlier in this chapter, I do think that there is a space for organizations in the metaverse for rehiring and creating continuous engagement with alumni.

Implementing the Metaverse

As with any other technology implementation, I would advise organizations to think about what goals the metaverse will help them achieve, what the expected ROI is, and why the organization is choosing to use the metaverse and for what reason. Sometimes, organizations look at all the problems that need to be solved as a technical issue, but actually it is a business and human problem, for which organizations need to set ground rules and establish ethics. New processes and protocols need to be determined, and organizations need to think about how to create a "responsible metaverse." HR will play a leading role in helping their organizations figure out how to make the best of this technology and how to make sure to make it beneficial for the employee experience. While there is tremendous potential, there are also risks to diversity and inclusion on multiple fronts.

- *Network access*: Not everywhere in the world do people have the same access to Internet bandwidth, and this could limit opportunities for individuals and thus have implications for their global teams. As technology advances, this might be resolved in the future.
- *Generational difference*: For the younger generation, working in the metaverse might feel more natural than for those of older generations.
- *Workplace safety*: One must determine how to avoid bullying, harassment, or other problematic behavior in the virtual world.
- *Physical abilities*: Some people cannot participate in VR due to physical limitations, such as vision impairment or circumstances that prevent them from being able to wear a headset.

The metaverse does allow employees to create idealized versions of themselves, and this could generate issues with people's self-esteem. A study on virtual tourism technologies examined reviews and blogs from individuals who tested virtual tourism and found that addiction and feelings of isolation occurred.[17] These effects could also apply when creating immersive experiences for employees and especially, the feeling of isolation could be considered a risk.

Case: Reducing Costs When Creating New Offices by Using the Metaverse

Jamie Fleming's background is in architecture and BIM modeling. In the past, when coordinating on projects, everything from a building's structure to its furnishings typically utilized a 2D workflow involving CAD drawings on paper, but now his team creates 3D models. One of their customers was actually my former employer, Microsoft, with which they collaborated on building the new headquarters for Microsoft Australia in Sydney. The project team was mainly based in Singapore and Seattle, Washington, and Jamie's team was in Bainbridge, Washington, while the stakeholders were in Sydney, Australia. The Altoura team loaded a virtual 3D model and, with their software, they hosted a meeting in that space as if it physically existed. People could actually walk through and interact with the space. Even though the people in Singapore were at their desks in Singapore and the people in Seattle were still in Seattle, they could join together and use avatars and Voice over IP (VoIP) to occupy the space. The technology is device-agnostic. It works on a phone, a tablet, a PC, or a HoloLens, or Meta Quest headset.

The iPhone's accelerometer allows for anchoring a 3D model in a physical space, and one can walk physically through a virtual world with every step normally taken in the physical world translating to the same step in the virtual world. The model can also be used like a video game and employees can tap on the screen and move around in the virtual world, as if they were moving in the physical world. One person could be on a phone, another could be on their PC, and a third could be using a headset, and they could all be together in the space and collaborate.

When the Microsoft and Altoura teams came together in the virtual space, the Microsoft project manager found many things wrong with the design, for example, a ceiling detail and other details that were not according to plan. The beauty was that with a 2D workflow, these details would never have been noticed until after the building's construction had been completed. Overall, the virtual walk-through, which allowed individuals to examine all of the details, spared the companies from many future change orders, because the problems were seen before construction. Correcting such issues is very expensive; 40 percent of construction costs often come from change orders alone. So, eliminating or drastically reducing them can make building 3D models worthwhile.

Conclusion

The metaverse represents a new opportunity for innovation in employee experience. It provides organizations with a unique opportunity to create immersive and engaging digital environments for their employees. However, whether or not an organization should use the metaverse for employee experiences depends on the intended outcome of the organizations, if it is worth the investment, and if employees can easily work with the technology. Organizations usually only want to make a significant capital investment in hardware, software, and the adoption and change processes associated with new technologies, if they understand what is at stake for the ROI potential of the technology. In other words, they want to know how much the new technology will save them.

On the one hand, the metaverse can provide a range of benefits for organizations, such as increased collaboration, improved productivity, and enhanced creativity. Being device-agnostic will make the metaverse more cost effective. The metaverse also has the potential to create a more diverse and inclusive workplace. On the other hand, there are also potential drawbacks to using the metaverse for employee experience. One concern is that it could lead to further isolation and disconnect among employees, particularly if they only work remotely. There are also potential privacy and security concerns. While the ROI for some cases is very clear, for others, it is still a work in progress.

Ultimately, whether or not an organization should use the metaverse for an enhanced employee experience will depend on careful considerations of its unique needs and goals. While the metaverse may not be the right fit for every organization (yet), those that choose to embrace the metaverse have the potential to create a truly innovative and engaging workplace that can drive productivity, creativity, and success. I do see the metaverse being used for more scenarios in HR and impacting organizational productivity as an improved employee experience. It is worth for organizations and HR departments to have a metaverse strategy in place to understand and consider the implications it has for their future workforce, making it a strategic choice if and when to enter the metaverse.

Conclusion

A common problem with determining the time horizon is that developments such as new technologies and innovations do not stick to dates. In 2000, many organizations did not yet include the rise of the smartphone in their strategic plans, while models were already being manufactured with which users could access the Internet, take photographs, and make purchases. These smartphone models were expensive and not available to everyone. Therefore, the impact of the smartphone was not within the scope of the strategic dialogue, but history shows us how quickly the smartphone rose to prominence and what impact it has had on what organizations do and the way they do it. Overall, the smartphone changed the way that organizations' employees work. Looking ahead and actively practicing IT and HR collaboration can help organizations understand what is next, what the implications are for their employees, and how the implications will affect the world of work.

It is crucial for organizations to have a strategy in place before deciding on what technologies to implement to enhance employee experience. HR teams need to collaborate closely with IT organizations to prevent a one-size-fits-all purchase. HR teams can assess individuals' and teams' needs and organizational boundaries, and accordingly, they can decide what the optimal technologies are to facilitate an optimal employee experience. Implementing new technologies without understanding how they fit within a business strategy, especially when organizations move to a hybrid working model, can prevent organizations from reaching their intended results. Ultimately, the goal is for employees and employers to be on the same page, finding a unique solution that suits the needs of both.

When implementing innovations, it is important that organizations research and realize the impact that these innovations have on its workforce. Interestingly, well-intended programs often do not work, because they are not rewarding for employees to use. When I interviewed Alex Bertram, who has spent his career in placing emerging technologies in the hands of frontline workers in the energy and resources industry, he made an appealing comparison. He compared implementing new technologies for employees with the experience that people had when they started using banking apps on their mobile devices. Nobody needed an extensive manual or assistance from a customer service agent to learn how the new mobile banking app worked. After clicking through a few screens, anyone could begin banking from a mobile device. Because it was so easy to use and better than the previous way of banking, it was quickly adopted and almost nobody went back to using legacy banking products. If organizations could make implementing new technologies for employees as rewarding and easy for employees, I expect an uptake in the adoption and usage of any program. The reality is that we are still making the implementation of new technologies for employees too complex. I would like to challenge organizations to think about how technology can help with creating a personalized employee experience and make new technologies worthwhile for employees to use.

New tools and technologies are constantly being developed that help organizations safeguard their skilled employees who help them become market leaders. The importance of employees' skills, particularly ethical and digital skills, cannot be overstated in today's rapidly evolving business landscape. Companies that invest in developing their employees' skills in these areas are more likely to be successful and maintain their market leadership positions. It is also important that employees are empowered not to just ask the tough questions, but also to find the tough answers. Exploring innovations, new technologies, and things we might think of as fictitious will have implications across security, marketing, customer relations, R&D, and beyond. It will be critical for organizations to have a consistent approach to decision making around big topics like security, privacy, safety, transparency, and ethical conduct. A useful starting point is to hold specific people or groups accountable for these answers and ensure that there are effective metrics to monitor the ongoing success and effects of any innovation.

New tools and technologies will continue to have a significant impact on employee well-being. Technology has enabled remote working opportunities and overall greater flexibility, which can improve work–life balance and reduce stress levels. On the other hand, constant connectivity and information overload brought about by new technologies can lead to burnout, anxiety, and a blurring of boundaries between employees' work and personal lives. When innovating and implementing new technologies, it is important for employers to recognize the potential negative effects and take steps to mitigate them. Organizations can also continue to look for technologies that promote employee well-being, which includes both the mental and physical health of employees. As the workplace continues to evolve, it will be important to strike a balance between leveraging the benefits of technology and prioritizing the health and well-being of employees.

As new innovations and technologies become more prevalent in the workplace, it is important to ensure that they are being developed and used fairly and without bias. This requires careful consideration of the design and implementation of AI tools, as well as ongoing monitoring and evaluation to identify and address any issues that may arise. Fairness in the use of AI tools at work is not only important from ethical and moral standpoints, but also helps to create a more inclusive and diverse workplace where all employees have an equal opportunity for success. By prioritizing fairness in the use of AI tools, organizations can unlock the full potential of these technologies while also promoting a more just and equitable society.

When innovating and looking for technologies to enhance employee experience, organizations should start with developments that will take place in the next one or two years, as relevant evidence and data already exist, and then expand the horizon to two to five years. The overall business strategy of the organization also often falls within this horizon, which often already includes developments and priorities that have an impact on the organization. Moreover, organizations can look even further to consider what will change in the next 5 to 15 years or even beyond. These considerations help to contextualize and sharpen strategic choices.

It may not always seem obvious how technology relates to HR or how these technologies translate to a better employee experience, but that is fine. It is important that IT and HR work together and stay curious. Exposing employees to new technologies and encouraging the workforce to experiment with them will help organizations in finding the right solutions to address their business challenges. Experimentations can be done in various ways: on an organizational level with, for example, a hackathon or on a broader level through regional or on an industry level through sectorwide experiments and learnings. I would also advise organizations not to wait and see how it all plays out; many of the technologies can be easily implemented. This means that organizations could become familiar with the technologies and create experiences that will help them to test technologies out at lower costs with smaller groups before making it available to all employees. It might also be the case that not all groups of employees need the same technologies, so creating personalized paths for different groups of employees contributes to a better employee experience and supports the business needs.

Often, the technology push is associated with improvements in an organization's product or services, but not with improvements in the internal processes that lead to higher productivity and more engaged and healthier employees. I will continue to encourage IT and HR to work more together and I hope you will join me on this journey, and together we will create the needed change to be more productive and increase well-being.

Notes

Chapter 1

1. Manyika, Lund, Chui, Bughin, Woetzel, Batra, Ko, and Sanghvi (2017).
2. Gartner on Gartner (2021).
3. Waters (2021).
4. Deloitte (2018).
5. McKinsey & Company (2020).
6. CBI Reports (2021).
7. LinkedIn Learning (2022).
8. Deloitte (2020).
9. Smith (2020).

Chapter 2

1. Kimbrough (2022).
2. Microsoft (2022).
3. Leaver (2022).
4. Microsoft (2022).
5. Gratton (2021).
6. Qatalog (2021).
7. Gartner on Gartner Newsroom (2021).
8. Farren (2023).
9. Statista (2023).
10. Coursera (2021).
11. Hollema (2020).

Chapter 3

1. Microsoft (2022).
2. Feigon and Block (2017).
3. Lifeworks.com (2019).

4. Herway (2020).

5. Dery and Sebastian (2017).

6. World Health Organization (2019).

7. Pfeffer (2018).

8. Business Wire (2017).

9. Microsoft (2020).

10. Deloitte (2018).

11. Green (2004), pp. 709–889.

12. Gallup (2022).

13. Deloitte (2022).

14. MacKay (2019).

15. Hirsch, Koch, and Karbach (2019).

16. Ramsøy (2019).

17. Fuller, Shikaloff, Cullinan, and Harmon (2018).

18. Cross, Taylor, and Zehner (2018).

19. Hunnicutt (1992), pp. 475–522.

20. Paul (2019).

21. PwC (2020).

22. Goel, Rao, Durner, and Dinges (2009).

23. van Dam and van der Helm (2016).

24. Gallup (2022).

25. Work Human Research Institute (2017).

26. Gartner (2021).

27. World Health Organization (2010).

Chapter 4

1. Dastin (2018).

2. Gender Insights Report (n.d.).

3. Mohr (2014).

4. Uwv.nl (2020).

5. Cook (n.d.).

6. Silverman (2015).

7. Uzzi (2019).

8. Catalyst (2014).

9. Vedantam (2023).
10. Attorneys for Plaintiffs Carolina Bernal Strifling and Willow Wren Turkal, on behalf of themselves and all others similarly situated United States District Court Northern District of California San Francisco Division Carolina Bernal Strifling and Willow Wren Turkal, on behalf of themselves and all others similarly situated (n.d.).
11. Bersin (2021).
12. Ibid.

Chapter 5

1. *Wall Street Journal* (2016).
2. People Analytics Trends Report (2021).
3. "Creating More Value With Your People Analytics Efforts Our Framework for Driving Value" (n.d.).
4. Pidgeon (2016).
5. Stoller (2021).
6. Kahneman (2012).
7. Heikkinen (2021).

Chapter 6

1. Gartner (2022).
2. Ball (2022).
3. Grieves (2016).
4. Alspach (2022).
5. "Work Trend Index: Microsoft's Latest Research on the Ways We Work" (2023).
6. Technavio (2022).
7. Samsung Biologics (2022).
8. PWC (2021).
9. Llarena (2013).
10. Gallup (2018).
11. Microsoft (2022).
12. Accenture (2022).

13. Business Wire (2022).

14. Future Workplace (2022).

15. Meister (n.d.).

16. Microsoft (2022).

17. Merkx and Nawijn (2021).

References

"Creating More Value With Your People Analytics Efforts Our Framework for Driving Value." n.d. *Pwc.nl*. www.pwc.nl/nl/actueel-publicaties/assets/pdfs/pwc-people-analytics-strategy.pdf.

"Work Trend Index: Microsoft's Latest Research on the Ways We Work." 2023. www.microsoft.com/en-us/worklab/work-trend-index/.

Accenture. 2022. *Get a Glimpse of the Metaverse Capabilities at Accenture*. www.youtube.com/watch?v=taRdfhRO9lY.

Alspach, K. January 26, 2022. "Why the Fate of the Metaverse Could Hang on Its Security." *VentureBeat*. https://venturebeat.com/uncategorized/why-the-fate-of-the-metaverse-could-hang-on-its-security/.

Attorneys for Plaintiffs Carolina Bernal Strifling and Willow Wren Turkal, on behalf of themselves and all others similarly situated United States District Court Northern District of California San Francisco Division Carolina Bernal Strifling and Willow Wren Turkal, on behalf of themselves and all others similarly situated. n.d. *Classaction.org*. www.classaction.org/media/bernal-et-al-v-twitter-inc.pdf.

Ball, M. 2022. *The Metaverse: And How It Will Revolutionize Everything*. New York, NY: WW Norton.

Bersin, J. 2021. *Elevating Equity and Diversity: The Challenge of the Decade*. https://joshbersin.com/2021/02/elevating-equity-and-diversity-the-challenge-of-the-decade.

Business Wire. 2017. *The Employee Burnout Crisis: Study Reveals Big Workplace Challenge in 2017*. www.businesswire.com/news/home/20170109005377/en/Employee-Burnout-Crisis-Study-Reveals-Big-Workplace.

Business Wire. 2022. *Toyota Material Handling Partners With VR Vision to Develop Training Resources Using Virtual Reality Technology*. www.businesswire.com/news/home/20220503005031/en/Toyota-Material-Handling-Partners-With-VR-Vision-to-Develop-Training-Resources-Using-Virtual-Reality-Technology.

Catalyst. 2014. *Coaches, Mentors, Sponsors: Understanding the Differences*. www.catalyst.org/research/infographic-coaches-mentors-and-sponsors-understanding-the-differences.

CBI reports 2021. *Developing Skills for Hybrid Working*. www.cbi.org.uk/media/7428/cbi-developing-skills-for-hybrid-working-2021.pdf.

Cook, I. n.d. "How HR Can Tackle Diversity Using the Rooney Rule." *Visier.com.* www.visier.com/blog/how-hr-can-tackle-diversity-using-the-rooney-rule/.

Coursera. 2021. *Impact Report.* https://about.coursera.org/press/wp-content/uploads/2021/11/2021-Coursera-Impact-Report.pdf.

Cross, R., S. Taylor, and D. Zehner. 2018. *Collaboration Without Burnout.* https://hbr.org/2018/07/collaboration-without-burnout.

Dastin, J. October 10, 2018. "Amazon Scraps Secret AI Recruiting Tool That Showed Bias Against Women." *Reuters.* www.reuters.com/article/us-amazon-com-jobs-automation-insight-idUSKCN1MK08G.

Deloitte. 2018. *Burnout Survey.* www2.deloitte.com/content/dam/Deloitte/us/Documents/about-deloitte/us-about-deloitte-burnout-survey-infographic.pdf.

Deloitte. 2018. *Future of Manufacturing: The Jobs Are Here, but Where Are the People?* www2.deloitte.com/us/en/pages/manufacturing/articles/future-of-manufacturing-skills-gap-study.html.

Deloitte. 2020. *Human Inside: How Capabilities Can Unleash Business Performance.* www2.deloitte.com/us/en/insights/focus/technology-and-the-future-of-work/building-capability-unleash-business-performance.html.

Deloitte. 2022. *Connectivity & Mobile Trends.* www2.deloitte.com/us/en/insights/industry/telecommunications/connectivity-mobile-trends-survey.html.

Dery, K. and I.M. Sebastian. 2017. *Building Business Value With Employee Experience.* www.avanade.com/-/media/asset/thinking/mit-research.pdf.

Farren, C. 2023. "Help New Hires Succeed: Beat the Statistics." *Thewynhurstgroup.com.* http://thewynhurstgroup.com/wp-content/uploads/2014/07/Help-New-Hires-Succeed.pdf (accessed May 11, 2023).

Feigon, M. and C.K. Block. 2017. *Work–Life Integration in Neuropsychology: A Review of the Existing Literature and Preliminary Recommendations.* www.researchgate.net/publication/321783056_Work-life_integration_in_neuropsychology_a_review_of_the_existing_literature_and_preliminary_recommendations.

Fuller, R., N. Shikaloff, R. Cullinan, and S. Harmon. January 25, 2018. "If You Multitask During Meetings, Your Team Will, Too." *Harvard Business Review.* https://hbr.org/2018/01/if-you-multitask-during-meetings-your-team-will-too.

Future Workplace. 2022. "VR Changes the Game for Soft Skills Training." *Futureworkplace.com.* https://futureworkplace.com/ebooks/vr-changes-the-game-for-soft-skills-training/.

Gallup. 2018. *State of the American workplace.* www.gallup.com/workplace/238085/state-american-workplace-report-2017.aspx.

Gallup. 2022. *State of the Global Workplace Report: 2022.* www.gallup.com/workplace/349484/state-of-the-global-workplace.aspx.

Gallup. 2022. *Unleashing the Human Element at Work: Transforming Workplaces Through Recognition*. www.gallup.com/analytics/392540/unleashing-recognition-at-work.aspx#ite-402182.

Gartner on Gartner Newsroom. 2021. *Gartner Survey Reveals a 44% Rise in Workers' Use of Collaboration Tools Since 2019*. www.gartner.com/en/newsroom/press-releases/2021-08-23-gartner-survey-reveals-44-percent-rise-in-workers-use-of-collaboration-tools-since-2019.

Gartner on Gartner Newsroom. February 4, 2021. *Press Release: Gartner HR Research Finds 58% of the Workforce Will Need New Skill Sets to Do Their Jobs Successfully*. www.gartner.com/en/newsroom/press-releases/2021-02-03-gartner-hr-research-finds-fifty-eight-percent-of-the-workforce-will-need-new-skill-sets-to-do-their-jobs-successfully.

Gartner, 2021. *Make Way for a More Human-Centric Employee Value Proposition*. www.gartner.com/smarterwithgartner/make-way-for-a-more-human-centric-employee-value-proposition.

Gartner. 2022. *Press Release: Garner Predicts 25% of People Will Spend at Least One Hour Per Day in the Metaverse by 2026*. www.gartner.com/en/newsroom/press-releases/2022-02-07-gartner-predicts-25-percent-of-people-will-spend-at-least-one-hour-per-day-in-the-metaverse-by-2026.

Gender Insights Report. n.d. *Linkedin.com*. https://business.linkedin.com/talent-solutions/diversity-inclusion-belonging/gender-balance-report.

Goel, N., H. Rao, J.S. Durner, and D.F. Dinges. 2009. *Neurocognitive Consequences of Sleep Deprivation*. www.ncbi.nlm.nih.gov/pmc/articles/PMC3564638.

Gratton, L. 2021. *How to Do Hybrid Right*. https://hbr.org/2021/05/how-to-do-hybrid-right.

Green, F. 2004. "Why Has Work Effort Become More Intense?" *Industrial Relations: A Journal of Economy and Society* 43, no. 4, pp. 709–889.

Grieves, M. 2016. *Origins of the Digital Twin Concept*. www.researchgate.net/publication/307509727_Origins_of_the_Digital_Twin_Concept/link/57c6f44008ae9d64047e92b4/download.

Heikkinen, I. 2021. *Graph Theory and the Six Degrees of Separation*. https://math.mit.edu/research/highschool/primes/circle/documents/2021/Heikkinen.pdf.

Herway, J. 2020. *Increase Productivity at the Lowest Possible Cost*. www.gallup.com/workplace/321743/increase-productivity-lowest-possible-cost.aspx.

Hirsch, P., I. Koch, and J. Karbach. 2019. *Putting a Stereotype to the Test: The Case of Gender Differences in Multitasking Costs in Task-Switching and Dual-Task Situations*. https://journals.plos.org/plosone/article?id=10.1371/journal.pone.0220150.

Hollema, T.S. 2020. *Virtual Teams Across Cultures: Create Successful Teams Around the World*. Interact Global.

Hunnicutt, B.K. 1992. "Kellogg's Six-Hour Day: A Capitalist Vision of Liberation Through Managed Work Reduction." *Business History Review* 66, no. 3, pp. 475–522.

Kahneman, D. 2012. *Thinking, Fast and Slow*. Harlow, England: Penguin Books

Kimbrough, K. 2022. *The Great Reshuffle in 2022: Top Trends to Watch*. www.linkedin.com/pulse/great-reshuffle-2022-top-trends-watch-karin-kimbrough.

Leaver, S. 2022. *Predictions 2023: Fortune Favors the Bold and Focused*. www.forrester.com/report/predictions-2023/RES178290.

Lifeworks.com. 2019. *Distressed Employees Ineffective for Eight Days Per Month Due to Lost Productivity*. https://lifeworks.com/en/news/distressed-employees-ineffective-eight-days-month-due-lost-productivity-0.

LinkedIn Learning 2022. *2022 Workplace Learning Report: The Transformation of L&D*. https://learning.linkedin.com/content/dam/me/learning/en-us/pdfs/workplace-learning-report/LinkedIn-Learning_Workplace-Learning-Report-2022-EN.pdf.

Llarena, M. 2013. "How Not to Lose Your New Employees in Their First 45 Days." *Forbes*. www.forbes.com/sites/85broads/2013/07/19/how-not-to-lose-your-new-employees-in-their-first-45-days.

MacKay, J. 2019. *Screen Time Stats 2019: Here's How Much You Use Your Phone During the Workday*. https://blog.rescuetime.com/screen-time-stats-2018/.

Manyika, J., S. Lund, M. Chui, J. Bughin, J. Woetzel, P. Batra, R. Ko, and S. Sanghvi. 2017. *What the Future of Work Will Mean for Jobs, Skills, and Wages*. McKinsey Global Institute. www.mckinsey.com/featured-insights/future-of-work/jobs-lost-jobs-gained-what-the-future-of-work-will-mean-for-jobs-skills-and-wages.

McKinsey & Company. 2020. *Beyond Hiring: How Companies Are Reskilling to Address Talent Gaps*. www.mckinsey.com/capabilities/people-and-organizational-performance/our-insights/beyond-hiring-how-companies-are-reskilling-to-address-talent-gaps.

Meister, J.C. n.d. *How Companies Are Using VR to Develop Employees' Soft Skills*. https://hbr.org/2021/01/how-companies-are-using-vr-to-develop-employees-soft-skills.

Merkx, C. and J. Nawijn. 2021. *Virtual Reality Tourism Experiences: Addiction and Isolation*. www.sciencedirect.com/science/article/pii/S0261517721001138.

Microsoft. 2020. *A Pulse on Employees' Wellbeing, Six Months Into the Pandemic*. www.microsoft.com/en-us/microsoft-365/blog/2020/09/22/pulse-employees-wellbeing-six-months-pandemic.

Microsoft. 2022. "Hybrid Work Is Just Work. Are We Doing It Wrong?" *Microsoft.com*. www.microsoft.com/en-us/worklab/work-trend-index/hybrid-work-is-just-work.

Microsoft. 2022. *Great Expectations: Making Hybrid Work Work*. www.microsoft.com/en-us/worklab/work-trend-index/great-expectations-making-hybrid-work-work.

Microsoft. 2022. *Hybrid Work Is Just Work. Are We Doing It Wrong?* www.microsoft.com/en-us/worklab/work-trend-index/hybrid-work-is-just-work.

Mohr, T.S. 2014. "Why Women Don't Apply for Jobs Unless They're 100% Qualified." *Harvard Business Review*. https://hbr.org/2014/08/why-women-dont-apply-for-jobs-unless-theyre-100-qualified.

Paul, K. 2019. *Microsoft Japan Tested a Four-Day Work Week and Productivity Jumped by 40%*. www.theguardian.com/technology/2019/nov/04/microsoft-japan-four-day-work-week-productivity.

People Analytics Trends Report. 2021. *Myhrfuture.com*. https://publications.myhrfuture.com/peopleanalyticstrends2021.

Pfeffer, J. 2018. *Dying for a Paycheck: How Modern Management Harms Employee Health and Company Performance—and What We Can Do About It*. HarperBusiness.

Pidgeon, C. 2016. "Know Your Focus Time at Work." *Workplace Insights*. https://workplaceinsights.microsoft.com/productivity/reclaiming-time-how-knowing-your-focus-time-at-work-can-restore-your-faith-in-humanity.

PwC. 2020. "Employee Financial Wellness Survey." www.pwc.com/us/en/services/consulting/business-transformation/library/financial-well-being-retirement-survey.html.

PWC. 2021. "Virtual Reality Recruitment." www.pwc.co.uk/who-we-are/annual-report/stories/2021/virtual-reality-recruitment.html.

Qatalog, 2021. *Workgeist Report '21*. https://assets.qatalog.com/language.work/qatalog-2021-workgeist-report.pdf.

Ramsøy, T.Z. September 10, 2019. "Pre-Crastination, Cognitive Demand, and Decisions." *Thomasramsoy.com*. https://thomasramsoy.com/index.php/2019/09/10/pre-crastination-cognitive-demand-and-decisions/.

Samsung Biologics. 2022. *Samsung Biologics Hosts Its First Metaverse Job Fair*. https://samsungbiologics.com/media/company-news-view?boardSeq=1642.

Silverman, R.E. 2015. "Gender Bias at Work Turns Up in Feedback." *Wall Street Journal* (East Ed). www.wsj.com/articles/gender-bias-at-work-turns-up-in-feedback-1443600759.

Smith, B. 2020. *Microsoft Launches Initiative to Help 25 Million People Worldwide Acquire the Digital Skills Needed in a COVID-19 Economy*. https://blogs.microsoft.com/blog/2020/06/30/microsoft-launches-initiative-to-help-25-million-people-worldwide-acquire-the-digital-skills-needed-in-a-covid-19-economy.

Statista. 2023. *Global Corporate e-Learning Market Size*. www.statista.com/statistics/1232427/global-corporate-e-learning-market-size/.

Stoller, K. 2021. "Companies Are Battling Burnout by Giving Employees More Vacation Days—but Will They Take Them?" *Forbes*. www.forbes.com/sites/kristinstoller/2021/05/19/companies-are-battling-burnout-by-giving-employees-more-vacation-days-but-will-they-take-them/?sh=73e53632267b.

Technavio. 2022. *Market Research Reports—Industry Analysis Size & Trends*. www.technavio.com/report/in-game-advertising-market-industry-analysis?u.

Uwv.nl. 2020. "Automonteurs Factsheet Arbeidsmarkt." www.uwv.nl/imagesdxa/automonteurs-factsheet-arbeidsmarkt_tcm94-447179.pdf.

Uzzi, B. 2019. "Research: Men and Women Need Different Kinds of Networks to Succeed." *Harvard Business Review*. https://hbr.org/2019/02/research-men-and-women-need-different-kinds-of-networks-to-succeed.

van Dam, N. and E. van der Helm. 2016. *The Organizational Cost of Insufficient Sleep*. www.mckinsey.com/capabilities/people-and-organizational-performance/our-insights/the-organizational-cost-of-insufficient-sleep?hlkid=d2905f8e3.

Vedantam, K. 2023. "The Crunchbase Tech Layoffs Tracker." *Crunchbase News*. https://news.crunchbase.com/startups/tech-layoffs/.

Wall Street Journal. 2016. "The Rise of Knowledge Workers Is Accelerating Despite the Threat of Automation." www.wsj.com/articles/BL-REB-35617.

Waters, S. 2021. "What Is a Skills Gap in Your Company? (Plus Gap Analysis Template)." *BetterUp*. www.betterup.com/blog/what-is-a-skills-gap.

Work Human Research Institute. 2017. *Bringing More Humanity to Recognition, Performance, and Life at Work*. www.workhuman.com/wp-content/uploads/2017/10/WHRI_2017SurveyReportA.pdf.

World Health Organization. 2010. *Healthy Workplaces: A Model for Action*. www.who.int/publications/i/item/9789241599313.

World Health Organization. 2019. *Burn-Out an "Occupational Phenomenon": International Classification of Diseases*. www.who.int/news/item/28-05-2019-burn-out-an-occupational-phenomenon-international-classification-of-diseases.

About the Author

Marlene de Koning is a director of HR Tech & Data at PwC, where she leads a team of HR tech and data specialists, who help clients drive workforce transformation, create data-driven strategies, and implement innovative technologies. She is also an author, a mentor for start-ups, an advocate for equality, and a public speaker. She lives in the Netherlands with her husband and two children.

Marlene has over 15 years of experience in the HR tech industry, and she has been at the forefront of digital transformation and employee experience. She was one of the first consultants at LinkedIn, bringing social media and talent solutions to the world of human resources. She was also part of Microsoft's Viva product engineering group, launching the first employee experience platform that integrates communication, learning, well-being, and insights.

Marlene is passionate about using data and technology to solve complex challenges and drive business success. She has written several articles about the top trends for employee experience, such as well-being, people analytics, employee skills, and hybrid work. She also mentors start-ups in the HR tech space and advocates for equality and diversity in the workplace.

Index

OTHER TITLES IN THE COLLABORATIVE INTELLIGIENCE COLLECTION

Jim Spohrer and Haluk Demirkan, Editors

- *The Edge Data Center* by Hugh Taylor
- *Journey to the Metaverse* by Antonio Flores-Galea
- *Doing Digital* by Ved Sen
- *Breakthrough* by Martin Fleming
- *How Organizations Can Make the Most of Online Learning* by David Guralnick
- *Teaching Higher Education to Lead* by Sam Choon-Yin
- *Business and Emerging Technologies* by George Baffour
- *How to Talk to Data Scientists* by Jeremy Elser
- *Leadership in The Digital Age* by Niklas Hageback
- *Cultural Science* by William Sims Bainbridge
- *The Future of Work* by Yassi Moghaddam, Heather Yurko, Haluk Demirkan, Nathan Tymann and Ammar Rayes
- *Advancing Talent Development* by Philip Gardner and Heather N. Maietta

Concise and Applied Business Books

The Collection listed above is one of 30 business subject collections that Business Expert Press has grown to make BEP a premiere publisher of print and digital books. Our concise and applied books are for…

- Professionals and Practitioners
- Faculty who adopt our books for courses
- Librarians who know that BEP's Digital Libraries are a unique way to offer students ebooks to download, not restricted with any digital rights management
- Executive Training Course Leaders
- Business Seminar Organizers

Business Expert Press books are for anyone who needs to dig deeper on business ideas, goals, and solutions to everyday problems. Whether one print book, one ebook, or buying a digital library of 110 ebooks, we remain the affordable and smart way to be business smart. For more information, please visit www.businessexpertpress.com, or contact sales@businessexpertpress.com.

www.ingramcontent.com/pod-product-compliance
Lightning Source LLC
Chambersburg PA
CBHW061215220326
41599CB00025B/4647